# Complete Book of Drills for Winning Baseball

## Cliff Ainsworth

**PRENTICE HALL**
Paramus, New Jersey 07652

**Library of Congress Cataloging-in-Publication Data**

Ainsworth, Cliff.
    Complete book of drills for winning baseball / Cliff Ainsworth.
      p.  cm.
    ISBN 0-13-089575-X (spiral wire)     ISBN 0-13-042580-X (paper)
    1. Baseball—Training.   2. Baseball—Coaching.  I. Title.

GV875.6 .A55  2001
796.357' 07' 7—dc21                          2001021528

©2001 by Prentice Hall

Acquisitions Editor: *Connie Kallback*
Production Editor: *Sharon L. Gonzalez*
Interior Design/Formatting: *Robyn Beckerman*

Printed in the United States of America

*10  9  8  7  6  5  4  3  2  1*              *10  9  8  7  6  5  4  3*

ISBN 0-13-089575-X (spiral wire)   ISBN 0-13-042580-X (paper)

**ATTENTION: CORPORATIONS AND SCHOOLS**

Prentice Hall books are available at quantity discounts with bulk purchase for educa-
tional, business, or sales promotional use. For information, please write to: Prentice Hall
Special Sales, 240 Frisch Court, Paramus, NJ 07652. Please supply: title of book, ISBN,
quantity, how the book will be used, date needed.

**PRENTICE HALL**
Paramus, NJ 07652

http://www.phdirect.com

*This book is dedicated first and foremost to endless deep blue skies.*
*Also to my heroes, Todd and Casey, the greatest children a father could ever want.*
*To Debbie, my wife of 25 years, for putting up with me for that long,*
*but especially for her love and support. And a special thanks of gratitude*
*to Bob G. and Jody for their unconditional friendships.*

# ABOUT THE AUTHOR

Cliff Ainsworth has been teaching for 23 years at Milton Hershey School, a private institution for needy children in Hershey, Pennsylvania. He is currently athletic director at the school, but he has taught fifth grade and ninth grade remedial language arts and was Learning Assistance Coordinator for 10 years.

Coach Ainsworth has coached high school baseball for 19 years, 15 years as head coach, and 4 years as an assistant. He resigned his head coaching position to be able to watch his son play his last 2 years of high school baseball and his daughter play high school softball. He then returned as assistant coach. During the summer months, he has also coached baseball from T-ball (5–7 year olds) to American Legion (16–18 year olds). In addition to coaching, he has run private pitching/batting instructional sessions with players from the community. His experience in other sports includes 23 years as assistant varsity football coach and 4 years coaching ninth-grade basketball.

# ABOUT THIS RESOURCE

I originally wrote this drill book for my coaching staff to use with the players in our baseball program. It represents a culmination of drills I have created or learned throughout my many years of coaching. After its completion, I felt there was a real need for such a resource and thought other coaches might benefit from its content.

The 238 easy-to-use drills in *Complete Book of Drills for Winning Baseball* epitomize the simplicity of learning and practicing basic skills of the game. Presented one per page for coaches to understand at a glance, the drills make the reinforcement of any skill simple and motivational because the sheer variety keeps players constantly interested and challenged.

The table of contents features the number and title of each drill and its purpose, which should prove to be a great planning tool for coaches at all levels. And the drills are arranged in a logical order into seven sections. Here's just a brief description of each section's contents:

Section 1, Infield, gives 53 drills from warming up to preparing players to field a variety of situations from ground balls to fly balls, double plays, run downs, holding the runner close and more.

The 30 drills in Section 2, Outfield, provide practice in running down and catching balls in a number of situations and conditions, such as times when the sun is directly in the outfielder's line of vision. The drills also emphasize techniques for catching, charging, scooping, and throwing the ball and, of utmost importance, communication between players.

Another 30 drills in Section 3, Pitching, range from getting the pitching arm ready (stretching, loosening and strengthening) to practicing and reinforcing various pitching motions, covering bases and reacting quickly during the game.

Section 4, Catching, presents 24 drills to help the pitcher develop skills in blocking, releasing, throwing, fielding, tagging and giving signals as well as reinforcing proper stance.

Combined Drills, the focus of section 5, gives a total of 34 drills for practice in communicating and covering wide-ranging situations such as coverage, pitcher to first base, cut-offs, tagging the runner in run downs and more.

Section 6, Batting, prepares players for up at bat through 44 drills that cover stance, mechanics of the swing, recognition of the strike zone, hand and arm position and techniques to meet all kinds of pitches.

Section 7, Base Running, features 23 drills for sliding, tagging up, stealing a base, recognizing signals, running with coach's instructions and timing.

My hope is that coaches ranging from Little League all the way to college level will find these drills as useful for implementation in their practice plans as I have through the years.

Cliff Ainsworth

# KEY TO SYMBOLS

P = Player or pitcher        R = Base runner
C = Catcher                  B = Batter
SS = Shortstop               RF = Right fielder
1B = First baseman           CF = Center fielder
2B = Second baseman          LR = Left fielder
3B = Third baseman           LHP = Left-handed pitcher
COACH = Coach                RHP = Right-handed pitcher

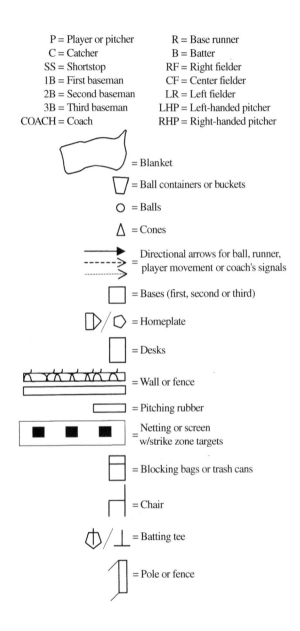

= Blanket

= Ball containers or buckets

= Balls

= Cones

= Directional arrows for ball, runner, player movement or coach's signals

= Bases (first, second or third)

= Homeplate

= Desks

= Wall or fence

= Pitching rubber

= Netting or screen w/strike zone targets

= Blocking bags or trash cans

= Chair

= Batting tee

= Pole or fence

# CONTENTS

## Section 1. Infield

1. Warm-Up Throwing . . . . . . . . . . . . *3*
   To loosen the throwing muscles; to practice the proper throwing and receiving techniques.

2. Relax, Ready, Move. . . . . . . . . . . . *4*
   To reinforce and practice readiness before and during the pitch, along with movement toward the ball.

3. Wave Drill. . . . . . . . . . . . . . . . *5*
   To develop a good stance, low body position and good lateral movement.

4. Ball Shuffle . . . . . . . . . . . . . . . *6*
   To develop lateral movement, proper fielding position and hand position as well as conditioning.

5. Circle Drill . . . . . . . . . . . . . . . *7*
   To reinforce the proper stance and good body and hand position.

6. Paired Form Fielding. . . . . . . . . . . *8*
   To develop and reinforce the proper stance, fielding position and foot movement when preparing to throw.

7. Proper Form Fielding . . . . . . . . . . *9*
   To develop and reinforce the proper stance, movement toward the ball, fielding and body position while throwing.

8. Soft Hands . . . . . . . . . . . . . . . *10*
   To develop and practice soft hands through repetition and proper fundamentals.

9. Back Hand. . . . . . . . . . . . . . . . *11*
   To develop and practice the skill of backhanding a ground ball and/or a thrown ball.

10. Four Corners. . . . . . . . . . . . . . *12*
    To develop quick feet, quick hands, glove and throwing hand relationship and proper throwing position of arm.

11. Bag Coverage . . . . . . . . . . . . . *13*
    To develop and practice the proper movement and positioning relative to the base while receiving a throw.

12. Cut-Off. . . . . . . . . . . . . . . . . *14*
    To develop the proper body, hand, arm and throwing position employed during a cut-off situation.

13. Ground Ball Mania . . . . . . . . . . . . *15*
    To practice the proper technique for fielding ground balls through maximum repetitions.

14. Fielding Bunts . . . . . . . . . . . . . . *16*
    To practice and reinforce the proper fielding technique when fielding a bunt.

15. Double Play Bag Work . . . . . . . . . . *17*
    To develop the proper receiving, footwork and throwing skills necessary to turn a double play.

16. Run-Down Line . . . . . . . . . . . . . *18*
    To practice and reinforce rotation during a run-down situation.

17. Fly Ball. . . . . . . . . . . . . . . . . *19*
    To develop the proper movement toward the ball, body position, foot position and throwing position.

18. Line Drive . . . . . . . . . . . . . . . *20*
    To develop movement toward the ball, the ability to field while moving and shifting the feet to throwing position after the catch.

19. Ground Ball Footwork . . . . . . . . . . *21*
    To get into position in front of the ball using the proper footwork.

20. Bad Hops. . . . . . . . . . . . . . . . *22*
    To reinforce the proper technique for fielding bad hops or bounces.

21. Relay Throws . . . . . . . . . . . . . . *23*
    To reinforce and develop the proper body position used to receive and throw during a relay situation.

22. Off-Balance Throws—On the Field . . . . *24*
    To practice off-balance throws to first base.

23. Off-Balance Throws—In the Gym . . . . . *25*
    To practice hurried, off-balance throws.

24. Bad Ball Drill at First Base. . . . . . . . *26*
    To practice fielding throws in the dirt.

25. Footwork at First Base . . . . . . . . . . . *27*
To practice and reinforce the proper footwork
at first base.

26. Fly Ball Drill—Catcher
and Third Baseman . . . . . . . . . . . . . *28*
To improve the chance of catching fly balls
down the third base line through better communication between the catcher and third
baseman.

27. Fly Ball Drill—Shortstop
and Second Baseman . . . . . . . . . . . *29*
To improve the chance of catching fly balls
in the middle infield through better communication between the shortstop and second
baseman.

28. Fly Ball Drill—Shortstop
and Third Baseman . . . . . . . . . . . . *30*
To improve the chance of catching fly balls
down the third base line through better communication between the shortstop and third
baseman.

29. Fly Ball Drill—First Baseman
and Second Baseman . . . . . . . . . . . *31*
To improve the chance of catching fly balls
down first base line through better communication between the first baseman and second
baseman.

30. Fly Ball Drill—Catcher and
First Baseman . . . . . . . . . . . . . . . *32*
To improve the chance of catching fly balls
down first base line through better communication between the catcher and first baseman.

31. Holding Runner Close—First Base . . . . *33*
To improve and reinforce techniques for holding the runner close to first base.

32. Holding Runner Close—Second Base . . . *34*
To improve and reinforce techniques for holding the runner close to second base.

33. Holding Runner Close—Third Base . . . . *35*
To improve and reinforce techniques for holding the runner close to third base.

34. Double Play Pivot—Shortstop . . . . . . *36*
To practice proper approach and footwork for
the shortstop turning a double play.

35. Double Play Pivot—Second Base . . . . . *37*
To practice the proper approach and footwork
for the second baseman turning a double play.

36. Backhand Toss—Second Base . . . . . . . *38*
To develop and practice the backhand toss by
the second baseman to the shortstop covering
second base.

37. Underhand Toss—Second Base . . . . . . *39*
To develop and practice the underhand toss
by the second baseman to the shortstop covering second base.

38. Jump-Pivot Toss—Second Base . . . . . . *40*
To develop and practice the jump-pivot toss
by the second baseman to the shortstop covering second base.

39. One-Knee Toss—Second Base . . . . . . . *41*
To develop and practice the one-knee toss by
the second baseman to the shortstop covering
second base.

40. Toss Combo Drill—Second Base . . . . . . *42*
To develop and practice the different tosses
used by the second baseman to the shortstop
covering second base.

41. Backhand Toss—Shortstop . . . . . . . . *43*
To develop and practice the backhand toss by
the shortstop to the second baseman covering
the base.

42. Underhand Toss—Shortstop . . . . . . . *44*
To develop and practice the underhand toss
by the shortstop to the second baseman covering the base.

43. One-Knee Toss—Shortstop . . . . . . . . *45*
To develop and practice the one-knee toss by
the shortstop to the second baseman covering
the base.

44. Sidearm Toss—Shortstop . . . . . . . . . *46*
To develop and practice the sidearm toss by
the shortstop to the second baseman covering
the base.

45. Toss Combo Drill—Shortstop . . . . . . . *47*
To develop and practice the different tosses
used by the shortstop to throw to the second
baseman covering the base.

46. Taking Throws at Second Base. . . . . . . *48*
To practice moving toward the second base
and receiving a throw from the catcher.

47. Taking Throws at Third Base . . . . . . . *49*
To practice moving toward third base and
receiving a throw from the catcher.

48. Third Baseman Making Throws to Second Base. . . . . . . . . . . . . . . *50*
    To practice and reinforce the third baseman making throws to second base.

49. First Baseman Making Throws to Second Base. . . . . . . . . . . . . . . *51*
    To practice and reinforce the first baseman making throws to second base.

50. Classroom Drill—Ready Position . . . . . *52*
    To reinforce the proper ready position before and during pitch delivery.

51. Classroom Drill—Fielding Position . . . . *53*
    To reinforce the proper fielding position while attacking a ground ball.

52. Classroom Drill—Initial Steps . . . . . . . *54*
    To practice the initial step when attacking a ground ball in the infield.

53. Charging the Ball . . . . . . . . . . . . . . *55*
    To practice charging a ground ball, reading the hop of the ball and playing through the ball.

# Section 2. Outfield

54. Long Toss . . . . . . . . . . . . . . . . . *59*
    To practice the proper throwing technique while strengthening the arm muscles.

55. Proper Fielding . . . . . . . . . . . . . . *60*
    To develop and reinforce proper fielding of ground balls and fly balls by outfielders.

56. Crow Hop . . . . . . . . . . . . . . . . . *61*
    To develop and practice the crow hop for gaining momentum at the beginning of the throwing motion.

57. Throwing to the Cut-Off Man . . . . . . *62*
    To practice and reinforce the technique of throwing the fielded ball to the cut-off man.

58. Fly Ball Communication . . . . . . . . . . *63*
    To reinforce the proper communication between outfielders while fielding a fly ball.

59. Gap Ball . . . . . . . . . . . . . . . . . . *64*
    To practice and reinforce the fielding technique needed to approach a ball in the gap.

60. Deep Ball. . . . . . . . . . . . . . . . . . *65*
    To practice running down and catching balls hit deep, whether in the gap or directly overhead.

61. Playing the Sun . . . . . . . . . . . . . . *66*
    To practice the technique of catching fly balls that require the fielder to look directly into the sun.

62. Charge—Scoop Drill . . . . . . . . . . . *67*
    To practice charging and scooping a ball hit to the outfield.

63. Charge, Scoop and Throw . . . . . . . . . *68*
    To practice charging, scooping and throwing the ball to prevent runners from taking extra bases.

64. Playing the Fence . . . . . . . . . . . . . *69*
    To practice catching fly balls and developing communication while playing balls hit near the fence.

65. Playing the Fence—Caroms/Bounces . . . *70*
    To practice fielding balls that carom or bounce off the outfield fence.

66. Playing the Fence—Combo. . . . . . . . . *71*
    To practice catching fly balls as well as playing caroms and bounces off the fence while developing communication between outfielders.

67. Sensational Catches. . . . . . . . . . . . . *72*
    To develop skill in turning and running for balls to the left, right or over your head.

68. Outfielders' Initial Steps . . . . . . . . . . *73*
    To develop the proper footwork on your initial reaction when tracking a ball to either side or directly behind you.

69. Outfielders' Footwork. . . . . . . . . . . . *74*
    To develop the proper footwork on your initial reaction when chasing a ball to either side or directly behind you.

70. Tag-Ups . . . . . . . . . . . . . . . . . . *75*
    To develop and reinforce the need to move forward through a fly ball while making a catch to gain the momentum needed to make a powerful throw.

71. One-Hop Drill . . . . . . . . . . . . . . . *76*
    To develop throwing long and low, one-hopping the ball to the bag.

72. Quick Start Drill. . . . . . . . . . . . . . . 77
To develop quick starts and movement toward
the ball in any direction.

73. Relay Off the Fence . . . . . . . . . . . . . 78
To practice throwing to the relay man or cut-off
after fielding a ball that bounced off the fence.

74. Ground Ball Drill (No One on Base). . . . 79
To reinforce skills needed when fielding a
ground ball in the outfield.

75. Ground Balls to Outfielders
Positioned in the Infield . . . . . . . . . . 80
To develop and practice the skill of fielding
ground balls.

76. Right-of-Way Drill . . . . . . . . . . . . 81
To practice and develop communication
between the outfielders.

77. Classroom—Initial Step . . . . . . . . . 82
To practice and reinforce the initial steps when
moving toward the ball in the outfield.

78. Classroom—Fly Ball Body Position . . . . 83
To practice the proper body position when
fielding fly balls.

79. Throws to the Bag. . . . . . . . . . . . . 84
To practice and reinforce throws to the
cut-off man and/or base.

80. Fly Balls to the Left . . . . . . . . . . . . 85
To practice catching fly balls to your left
while on the run.

81. Fly Balls to the Right . . . . . . . . . . 86
To practice catching fly balls to your right
while on the run.

82. Ground Balls to the Left . . . . . . . . . 87
To practice fielding ground balls to your left
while on the run.

83. Ground Balls to the Right . . . . . . . . 88
To practice fielding ground balls to your
right while on the run.

# Section 3.  Pitching

84. Long Toss . . . . . . . . . . . . . . . . . 91
To loosen, strengthen and stretch the
throwing arm.

85. Five-Step Drill. . . . . . . . . . . . . . . 92
To practice and reinforce the proper technique
throughout each phase of the pitching motion.

86. One-Knee Follow-Through . . . . . . . . 93
To practice and reinforce the proper follow
through after the release of the ball.

87. Balance While Throwing . . . . . . . . . 94
To practice and reinforce the balance/power
position during the pitching motion.

88. Towel Drill. . . . . . . . . . . . . . . . . 95
To reinforce the wrist snap and follow
through during the pitching motion.

89. Target Drill . . . . . . . . . . . . . . . . 96
To develop accuracy when pitching and
spotting the ball in the strike zone.

90. Bag Drill . . . . . . . . . . . . . . . . . 97
To develop accuracy and comfort throwing
with a batter standing in the batter's box.

91. Preseason Throwing. . . . . . . . . . . . 98
To strengthen and develop the pitcher's arm
leading up to the season.

92. Pick-Off Options. . . . . . . . . . . . . . 99
To practice options when holding a runner
close to first base.

93. Fielding Bunts . . . . . . . . . . . . . . 100
To practice and reinforce the proper fielding
and throwing techniques for pitchers coming
off the mound to field bunts.

94. Spin Drill . . . . . . . . . . . . . . . . . 101
To practice and reinforce placing the proper
spin on the ball for different pitches.

95. Backing Up Bases . . . . . . . . . . . . 102
To practice backing up throws to second
base, third base and home plate.

96. Follow-Through Drill . . . . . . . . . . . 103
To practice and reinforce follow through during the pitching motion.

97. Covering First Base . . . . . . . . . . . . 104
To practice first base coverage by the pitcher
on a ball hit to the right side of the infield.

98. Covering Bases on Fly Balls. . . . . . . *105*
To reinforce base coverage by the pitcher on
a fly ball to the infield.

99. Comeback Ball—Throwing to First . . . *106*
To practice throwing the ball to first base on
a comeback ball hit to the pitcher.

100. Comeback Ball—Throwing to
Second Base . . . . . . . . . . . . . . . *107*
To practice throwing the ball to second base
on a comeback hit to the pitcher.

101. Premature Break by Base Runner . . . . *108*
To practice and reinforce defending against a
premature break by a base runner.

102. Premature Break by Base Runner—
First and Third . . . . . . . . . . . . . . *109*
To practice and reinforce defending against a
premature break by a base runner during a first
and third situation.

103. Bunt Reaction Drill . . . . . . . . . . . *110*
To practice fielding bunts and throwing to
different bases.

104. Curve Ball Drill . . . . . . . . . . . . . *111*
To practice putting the proper spin on the
curve ball.

105. Double Bunt Drill . . . . . . . . . . . . *112*
To practice fielding bunts and throwing to
first or third base.

106. Running Foul Poles . . . . . . . . . . . *113*
To warm up as well as condition the pitchers
before the game and during practice.

107. Double Ball Drill . . . . . . . . . . . . . *114*
To condition pitchers during the preseason
as well as in-season.

108. Slide-Step Drill . . . . . . . . . . . . . *115*
To practice and reinforce the slide step by
the pitcher during the stretch motion.

109. Spot Drill . . . . . . . . . . . . . . . . . *116*
To practice spotting the baseball in different
locations in the strike zone.

110. Situational Pitching . . . . . . . . . . . *117*
To practice throwing different types of pitches
to different locations and from the windup or
stretch, all being dictated by the situation.

111. Wall Drill . . . . . . . . . . . . . . . . . *118*
To practice the backward reach of the
pitcher during the pitching motion.

112. Hand-Break Drill . . . . . . . . . . . . . *119*
To reinforce and coordinate the hand break
with the stride to home, keeping the body
together during the pitching motion.

113. Chair Drill . . . . . . . . . . . . . . . . . *120*
To reinforce the follow-through by the
pitcher during the pitching motion.

# Section 4.  Catching

114. Blocking Drill—No Hands . . . . . . . . *123*
To develop and reinforce the proper blocking
technique without using hands when the ball
is thrown in the dirt.

115. Blocking Drill—Ball in Front . . . . . . *124*
To develop and reinforce the proper blocking
technique when the ball is thrown in the dirt
in front of the catcher.

116. Blocking Drill—Balls to the
Left or Right . . . . . . . . . . . . . . . *125*
To develop and reinforce the proper blocking
technique when the ball is thrown in the dirt
to the left or to the right of the catcher.

117. Blocking Drill—Throwing to Bases. . . . *126*
To develop and reinforce the proper blocking
technique when the ball is in the dirt and a
throw to a base is required.

118. Release Drill . . . . . . . . . . . . . . . *127*
To develop and reinforce the catcher's stance
to allow releasing the ball with quickness.

119. Foul Ball . . . . . . . . . . . . . . . . . *128*
To develop and reinforce the proper technique
for fielding foul pop-ups behind home plate.

120. Throws to First Base. . . . . . . . . . . *129*
To reinforce and practice throws to first base
from behind the plate.

121. Throws to Third Base . . . . . . . . . . *130*
To reinforce and practice throws to third
base from behind the plate.

122. Fielding Bunts . . . . . . . . . . . . . . *131*
To reinforce and practice the catcher's ability
to field a bunted ball.

123. Fielding Bunts—Throwing to
First Base . . . . . . . . . . . . . . . . . *132*
To reinforce and practice fielding a bunted
ball and then throwing to first base.

124. Fielding Bunts—Throwing to
Second Base . . . . . . . . . . . . . . *133*
To reinforce and practice fielding a bunted ball
and then throwing to second base.

125. Fielding Bunts—Throwing to
Third Base . . . . . . . . . . . . . . . . *134*
To reinforce and practice fielding a bunted
ball and then throwing to third base.

126. Setup Drill—Classroom . . . . . . . . . *135*
To reinforce the proper stance of the catcher
during the game.

127. Setup Drill . . . . . . . . . . . . . . . . *136*
To reinforce the proper stance of the catcher
during the game.

128. Signal Drill . . . . . . . . . . . . . . . . *137*
To practice giving signals so they can be
seen only by the pitcher.

129. Throwing Drill . . . . . . . . . . . . . . . *138*
To practice gripping the ball properly while
throwing.

130. Backup Drill—Third Base . . . . . . . *139*
To practice backing up third base during a
bunt situation when the third baseman fields
the ball with a runner on first base.

131. Backup Drill—First Base . . . . . . . . *140*
To practice backing up first base on a ball
thrown to first base with no runner on base.

132. Tag Drill . . . . . . . . . . . . . . . . . . *141*
To practice blocking home plate and making
the tag on a runner attempting to score.

133. Third Strike Drill . . . . . . . . . . . . . *142*
To practice having the catcher react to a
dropped third strike by either tagging the
batter or throwing the ball to first base.

134. Wide Pitch Drill . . . . . . . . . . . . . . *143*
To practice stepping out to receive a pitch wide
out of the strike zone.

135. Bases Loaded Drill . . . . . . . . . . . . . *144*
To practice and reinforce the footwork by the
catcher at home plate when bases are loaded.

136. Pop-Up Drill . . . . . . . . . . . . . . . . *145*
To practice catching pop-ups.

137. Passed Ball Drill . . . . . . . . . . . . . *146*
To practice and reinforce retrieving a ball
that has gotten past the catcher, then tossing
the ball to the pitcher covering home plate.

# Section 5.  Combined Drills

138. Pitcher/First Base Coverage . . . . . . . *149*
To develop and reinforce the proper
technique for the pitcher covering first
base; the proper presentation and throwing
of the ball by first baseman to the pitcher
covering bag.

139. Fly Ball Communication—Left Fielder,
Third Baseman and Shortstop . . . . . . *150*
To practice communication between the left
fielder, third baseman and shortstop on fly
balls, while reinforcing fielding techniques
for each position.

140. Fly Ball Communication—Center Fielder,
Shortstop and Second Baseman . . . . . *151*
To practice communication between the
center fielder, second baseman and shortstop
on fly balls, while reinforcing fielding
techniques for each position.

141. Fly Ball Communication—Right Fielder,
First Baseman and Second Baseman . . . *152*
To practice communication between the right
fielder, first baseman and second baseman
on fly balls, while reinforcing fielding
techniques for each position.

142. Home Plate Coverage . . . . . . . . . . . *153*
To practice pitcher and catcher communication and coverage of home plate during a passed ball or wild pitch situation.

143. **Run Down Between First Base and Second Base** . . . . . . . . . . . . . *154*
To practice and reinforce the proper technique and positioning during a run-down situation between first and second base.

144. **Run Down Between Second Base and Third Base** . . . . . . . . . . . . . . *155*
To practice and reinforce the proper technique and positioning during a run-down situation between second and third base.

145. **Run Down Between Third Base and Home Plate** . . . . . . . . . . . . . *156*
To practice and reinforce the proper technique and positioning during a run-down situation between third base and home plate.

146. First and Third . . . . . . . . . . . . . . *157*
To practice and develop ways to defend the first and third situation by using different options/plays.

147. Holding Runners Close—First Base . . . *158*
To practice and reinforce holding runners close to first base, as well as proper timing during pick-off plays.

148. Holding Runners Close—Second Base . . *159*
To practice and reinforce holding runners close to second base, as well as proper timing during pick-off plays.

149. Holding Runners Close—Third Base . . . *160*
To practice and reinforce holding runners close to third base, as well as proper timing during pick-off plays.

150. Three-Ring Circus . . . . . . . . . . . . . *161*
To involve three separate infield drills within the infield.

151. Bunt Coverage . . . . . . . . . . . . . . . *162*
To practice and fine-tune bunt coverage movements, as well as fielding techniques during those movements.

152. Cut-Offs . . . . . . . . . . . . . . . . . . *163*
To practice and reinforce not only the proper throwing technique by outfielders, but also the proper cut-off positioning, bag coverage and communication by infielders.

153. Extra Base Cut-Offs . . . . . . . . . . . . *164*
To practice and reinforce not only the proper throwing technique by outfielders, but also the proper extra base cut-off positioning, bag coverage and communication by infielders.

154. Cut-Offs with Runners . . . . . . . . . . *165*
To practice and reinforce not only the proper throwing technique by outfielders, but also the proper cut-off positioning, bag coverage and communication by infielders with runners on base.

155. Cut-Offs with Runner Tagging . . . . . . *166*
To practice and reinforce not only the proper throwing technique by outfielders, but also the proper cut-off positioning, bag coverage and communication by infielders with runners tagging up at a base.

156. **Throws to Second Base— Third Baseman** . . . . . . . . . . . . . . *167*
To practice and reinforce having the third baseman throw the ball to second base for a force play or the start of a double play.

157. **Throws to Second Base— First Baseman** . . . . . . . . . . . . . . *168*
To practice and reinforce having the first baseman throw the ball to second base for a force play or the start of a double play.

158. **Throws to Second Base—The Pitcher** . . *169*
To practice and reinforce having the pitcher throw the ball to second base for a force play or the start of a double play.

159. Infield/Outfield—Outfield Segment . . . *170*
To practice and reinforce not only the proper throwing technique by outfielders, but also the proper cut-off positioning, bag coverage and communication by infielders.

160. Infield/Outfield—Infield Segment . . . . *171*
To practice the proper fielding technique and throws to bases by infielders.

161. Situations—Full Defense . . . . . . . . . *173*
To practice and reinforce situations that may occur during a game, such as cut-off movement, bunt coverage, first and third, pitcher covering first base, defensively as well as offensively.

162. Situations—Infield Only . . . . . . . . . *174*
To practice and reinforce situations that may occur in the infield during a game, defensively as well as offensively.

163. Batting Practice—Field Setup I . . . . . *175*
To make efficient use of players and field
space while reinforcing fielding skills as
well as batting skills.

164. Batting Practice—Field Setup II . . . . . *176*
To make efficient use of players and field
space while reinforcing fielding skills as
well as batting skills.

165. Live Sacrifice Bunt. . . . . . . . . . . . . *177*
To practice and reinforce the bunt technique
versus live pitching.

166. Live Bunting for a Base Hit . . . . . . . . *178*
To practice and reinforce the bunt technique
versus live pitching

167. Live Combo Bunt Drill . . . . . . . . . . *179*
To practice and reinforce the bunt technique
versus live pitching.

168. Pride Drill . . . . . . . . . . . . . . . . . *180*
To develop team pride and conditioning by
running on and off the field.

169. Pepper Drill . . . . . . . . . . . . . . . . *181*
To reinforce hand/eye coordination as well
as quickness and agility.

170. Pregame Drill. . . . . . . . . . . . . . . . *182*
To reinforce defensive situations prior to the
start of the game.

171. All Purpose Drill . . . . . . . . . . . . . . *183*
To reinforce defensive situations that might
arise during the game.

# Section 6.  Batting

172. Classroom Stance and
Alignment Drill . . . . . . . . . . . . . *187*
To develop the proper stance and good
alignment when in the batter's box.

173. Classroom Load Drill . . . . . . . . . . *188*
To develop the load, keeping the hands and
weight back to prepare the body for the
swing.

174. Classroom Swing Drill. . . . . . . . . . *189*
To develop and practice the proper swing
mechanics.

175. Classroom One-Arm
Swing Drill—Front Hand . . . . . . . . *190*
To develop and practice the proper mechanics
of the swing using only the front hand.

176. Classroom One-Arm
Swing Drill—Back Hand . . . . . . . . *191*
To develop and practice the proper mechanics
of the swing using only the back hand.

177. Isometric Swing Drill . . . . . . . . . . *192*
To strengthen the muscles involved in the
swing.

178. Weighted Bat Drill. . . . . . . . . . . . . *193*
To strengthen the muscles involved in the
swing.

179. Strike Zone Drill . . . . . . . . . . . . . *194*
To develop the recognition of pitches in the
strike zone.

180. Load Drill. . . . . . . . . . . . . . . . . . *195*
To practice the load, keeping the hands and
weight back to prepare the body for the swing.

181. Mirror Drill. . . . . . . . . . . . . . . . . *196*
To analyze the mechanics of the batter's swing.

182. Hip Drill . . . . . . . . . . . . . . . . . . *197*
To develop and reinforce the proper hip
rotation during the swing.

183. Towel Drill . . . . . . . . . . . . . . . . . *198*
To develop and reinforce hand quickness during
the swing to the point of contact with the ball.

184. Rolled-Up Towel Drill . . . . . . . . . . . *199*
To reinforce the back arm position prior to
and during the swing.

185. Single-Arm Towel Drill—Back Hand . . *200*
To develop and reinforce backhand quickness
during the swing to the point of contact with
the ball.

186. Single-Arm Towel Drill—Front Hand . . *201*
To develop and reinforce front hand quickness
during the swing to the point of contact with
the ball.

187. Throw Drill. . . . . . . . . . . . . . . . . *202*
To reinforce the proper hand position and
movement toward the ball during the swing.

188. Flip-Toss Drill . . . . . . . . . . . . . . . *203*
To practice and reinforce the proper hitting
technique, which involves feet, hands,
weight, stride and swing.

189. Flip-Toss Drill—Hitting
the Inside Pitch. . . . . . . . . . . . . . 204
To practice and reinforce the proper hitting
mechanics for a pitch on the inside part of
the plate.

190. Flip-Toss Drill—Hitting
the Outside Pitch. . . . . . . . . . . . . 205
To practice and reinforce the proper hitting
mechanics for a pitch on the outside part of
the plate.

191. Flip-Toss Drill—Lead Hand Swing. . . . 206
To reinforce the mechanics of the lead hand
moving toward the contact point during the
swing.

192. Flip-Toss Drill—Back Hand Swing. . . . 207
To reinforce the mechanics of the back hand
moving toward the contact point during the
swing.

193. Flip-Toss–Slap Drill . . . . . . . . . . . 208
To reinforce the hand movement toward the
ball during the swing.

194. Flip-Toss–Two-Ball Drill . . . . . . . . 209
To develop concentration on the contact
point during the swing.

195. Flip-Toss–Numbered Ball Drill . . . . . 210
To develop concentration on the contact
point during the swing.

196. Flip-Toss Drill from Behind. . . . . . . 211
To develop hand quickness to the point of
contact with the ball.

197. Batting Tee Drill . . . . . . . . . . . . . 212
To develop and reinforce the proper hitting
mechanics.

198. Batting Tee—Lead Hand Swing . . . . . 213
To reinforce the mechanics of the lead hand
moving toward the contact point during the
swing.

199. Batting Tee—Back Hand Swing . . . . . 214
To reinforce the mechanics of the back hand
moving toward the contact point during the
swing.

200. Batting Tee Drill—Hitting
the Inside Pitch. . . . . . . . . . . . . . 215
To practice the proper mechanics when
hitting an inside pitch.

201. Batting Tee Drill—Hitting
the Outside Pitch. . . . . . . . . . . . . 216
To practice the proper mechanics when
hitting an outside pitch.

202. Double Tee Drill . . . . . . . . . . . . . 217
To practice the slight downward angle of the
bat during the swing as the bat approaches
the contact point.

203. Walk-Through Drill . . . . . . . . . . . 218
To reinforce keeping the weight and hands
back prior to the swing.

204. Drop Drill. . . . . . . . . . . . . . . . . 219
To develop quick hands through the
strike zone by using the proper swing
technique.

205. Drop Drill—Whiffle Golf Balls . . . . . 220
To develop quick hands through the strike
zone by using the proper swing technique.

206. Bounce Drill . . . . . . . . . . . . . . . 221
To reinforce keeping the hands and weight
back during the swing.

207. Whiffle Golf Ball Drill. . . . . . . . . . 222
To develop focus and concentration on the
ball through the strike zone.

208. Whiffle Golf Ball Drill—
Broom Stick . . . . . . . . . . . . . . . 223
To develop focus and concentration on the
ball through the strike zone.

209. Dry Swing . . . . . . . . . . . . . . . . 224
To reinforce the proper hitting mechanics,
which include the stance, step, swing and
rhythm.

210. Compact Swing . . . . . . . . . . . . . 225
To develop and reinforce the hand and arm
position involved in creating a compact
swing.

211. Mime Bunt . . . . . . . . . . . . . . . . 226
To practice and reinforce the proper
movement, body position and technique
involved in bunting.

212. Bunt Teams. . . . . . . . . . . . . . . . 227
To practice and reinforce proper movement,
body position and technique, as well as the
bunt itself.

213. Bucket Drill . . . . . . . . . . . . . . . 228
To develop the skill of bunting the ball down
the first and third base lines.

214. Close-Quarter Batting Practice . . . . . 229
To make batting practice more efficient.

215. Batting Practice with a Purpose . . . . . 230
To reinforce hitting mechanics, also to
develop situational thinking while hitting.

# Section 7. Base Running

216. Crossover Drill . . . . . . . . . . . . . . . *233*
To develop the proper initial step from a lead stance when advancing to another base.

217. Sliding Drill . . . . . . . . . . . . . . . *234*
To develop and practice the sliding technique when approaching a base.

218. Tagging Up Drill—First and Second Base . . . . . . . . . . . . . . . *235*
To practice tagging up on a fly ball hit to the outfield.

219. Tagging Up Drill—Third Base . . . . . . *236*
To practice tagging up on a fly ball hit to the outfield.

220. Tip-Off Drill—Right-Handed Pitcher . . *237*
To practice recognizing signals from a right-handed pitcher that tip off the base runner.

221. Stealing Drill . . . . . . . . . . . . . . . *238*
To practice taking a lead and stealing a base.

222. Tip-Off Drill—Left-Handed Pitcher . . . *239*
To practice recognizing signals from a left-handed pitcher that tip off the base runner.

223. First Base Turn Drill—Veer Out . . . . . *240*
To reinforce the proper mechanics while making a turn at first base.

224. First Base Turn Drill—Extra Base Hit . . . . . . . . . . . . . . . *241*
To reinforce the proper mechanics while making a turn at first base.

225. First Base Turn Drill—Aggressive Turns . . . . . . . . . . . . . . . *242*
To reinforce the proper mechanics while making an aggressive turn at first base.

226. Circuit Running . . . . . . . . . . . . . . . *243*
To reinforce proper base running, while incorporating conditioning.

227. Leads at First Base . . . . . . . . . . . . . . . *244*
To reinforce and practice taking leads off first base and recognizing the pitcher's initial movement.

228. Leads at Second Base . . . . . . . . . . . . *245*
To reinforce and practice taking leads off second base as well as visual cues from the pitcher.

229. Leads at Third Base . . . . . . . . . . . . *246*
To reinforce and practice running leads from third, as well as instantly recognizing a fly ball or a ground ball.

230. Home to Second Base . . . . . . . . . . . *247*
To practice running from home to second base with the first base coach's direction.

231. Home to Third Base . . . . . . . . . . . . *248*
To practice running from home plate to third base with base coach's instructions.

232. Second Base to Home . . . . . . . . . . . *249*
To practice running from second base to home with a coach's instructions.

233. First Base to Third Base . . . . . . . . . *250*
To practice running from first to third base with a coach's instructions.

234. First and Third Drill . . . . . . . . . . . *251*
To practice the timing of the runner on third base breaking toward home on the catcher's throw to second base.

235. Bunt and Run Drill . . . . . . . . . . . . *252*
To practice the base runner's timing during a bunt play.

236. Squeeze Drill . . . . . . . . . . . . . . . *253*
To practice the base runner's timing during a squeeze bunt play.

237. Suicide Squeeze Drill . . . . . . . . . . . *254*
To practice the base runner's timing during a suicide squeeze play.

238. Two Outs—Full Count Drill. . . . . . . *255*
To practice the two outs, full count situation with base runners.

# SECTION 1

# INFIELD

*In order to succeed we must first believe we can.*

—MICHAEL KORDA

# 1. Warm-Up Throwing

**Primary Skill:** Throwing

**Objective:** To loosen the throwing muscles; to practice the proper throwing and receiving techniques.

**Equipment Needed:** One baseball for each pair of players

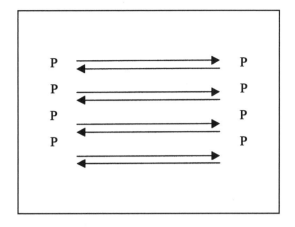

## COACH

• Circulate on both sides of the drill, monitoring the players as they throw and making corrections as needed.

• This is a vital part of practice. Make sure the players understand the importance of this activity.

• Make sure pairs are all throwing in the same direction. This is safer and easier to monitor.

• Monitor throws from a short distance. Remind the players to gradually move to longer throws. Long throwing will strengthen and stretch the arms.

## PLAYER

• Pair up, initially standing 10 yards apart.

• Use a complete follow-through motion.

• Take 10 to 12 throws from a short distance, and then move back three steps while continuing throwing motion.

• Receive the ball by reaching with both hands. Practice receiving and quick release from the glove.

**NOTE:** Prior to starting the drill, jog two laps around the field to break a sweat and increase heart rate.

# 2. Relax, Ready, Move

**Primary Skill:** Agility, defensive body positioning

**Objective:** To reinforce and practice readiness before and during the pitch, along with movement toward the ball.

**Equipment Needed:** None

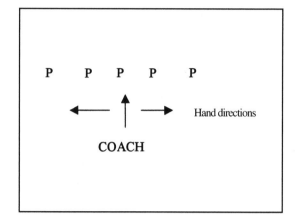

## COACH

- Give the players a verbal cue or visual signal to get them into a readiness position.
- Next, give the players a direction left, right or forward. Use a pitching motion for readiness and movement.

## PLAYER

- Wait for the coach's cue to get into a readiness position. Focus on the pitching motion to get into a readiness position.
- Move on the coach's next direction, left, right or forward for two to three steps.

**NOTE:** This drill can be used on the diamond with the infielders and the outfielders simultaneously.

# 3. Wave Drill

**Primary Skill:** Agility

**Objective:** To develop a good stance, low body position and good lateral movement.

**Equipment Needed:** None

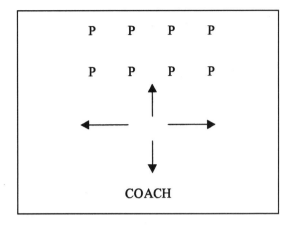

## COACH

• Give the players directions by using hand motions left, right, forward and backward.

## PLAYER

• Feet should be at least shoulder width, on toes, knees bent, butt down.

• Hands are on the ground in front of the body.

• Shuffle the feet following the coach's hand signals left, right, forward and backward.

*Variation:* Use a crossover step, to the left or to the right.

# 4. Ball Shuffle

**Primary Skill:** Agility

**Objective:** To develop lateral movement, proper fielding position and hand position as well as conditioning.

**Equipment Needed:** Three or four baseballs

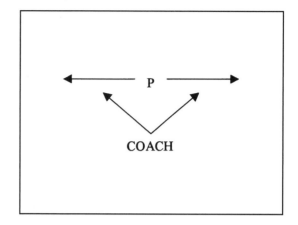

## COACH

- Roll the first ball approximately 5 to 10 feet to the player's left or right.
- As soon as the ball is being flipped back, roll the next ball in the opposite direction.
- Speed and distance of the ball should be regulated.

## PLAYER

- Get into the proper stance with the feet shoulder width, on toes, knees bent, butt low.
- Place the hands out in front, on the ground.
- As the ball is rolled, shuffle to the ball, staying in position. Field the ball and flip back to the coach while getting ready for the next ball.

# 5. Circle Drill

**Primary Skill:** Stance, hand and body position

**Objective:** To reinforce the proper stance and good body and hand position.

**Equipment Needed:** One baseball

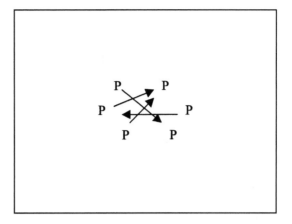

## COACH

• Monitor the circle for the proper stance with hands out in front and on the ground.

• Be a part of the circle to demonstrate the technique.

## PLAYER

• Form a circle with little or no space between players while maintaining a proper stance.

• Both hands should be on the ground in front of the body.

• Roll the ball across the circle to another player, who in turn slaps or pushes the ball to someone else.

• The objective is to try to slap the ball through another player's legs.

• Continue this routine until someone misses the ball, rest and then regroup to start over again.

**NOTE:** Start slowly to emphasize good form, gradually increasing the speed of the ball in the circle to develop quicker hands.

# 6. Paired Form Fielding

**Primary Skill:** Stance, fielding position and foot movement

**Objective:** To develop and reinforce the proper stance, fielding position and foot movement when preparing to throw.

**Equipment Needed:** One baseball per pair

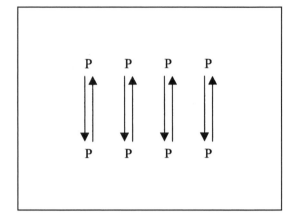

## COACH

- Demonstrate the proper fielding technique prior to the drill.
- Monitor the repetitions, stressing quality.

## PLAYER

- Pair up facing each other.
- One player starts with the ball and rolls it to the partner at a comfortable fielding speed.
- Use good form when receiving the ball, followed by quick foot movement in preparation to throw; everything is done to throw the ball except the release.
- The receiver of the ball now becomes the roller.
- Repeat the above—it's important to stress quality not quantity of the repetitions.

# 7. Proper Form Fielding

**Primary Skill:** Proper fielding

**Objective:** To develop and reinforce the proper stance, movement toward the ball, fielding and body position while throwing.

**Equipment Needed:** A bag of baseballs and gloves

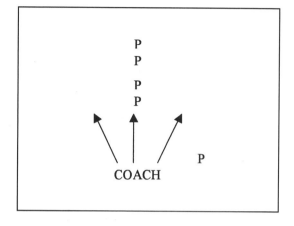

## COACH

- Stand about 15 to 20 yards from the players, throw ground balls directly at the players, check for the proper fielding position, eventually throwing the balls to the left then to the right. Give each player three repetitions.

## PLAYER

- Start in a good ready position, move toward the ball, get into the proper fielding position.
- Field the ball, funneling it to the navel.
- Get the body into throwing position and throw the ball to the player next to the coach.

# 8. Soft Hands

**Primary Skill:** Soft hands

**Objective:** To develop and practice soft hands through repetition and proper fundamentals.

**Equipment Needed:** A bag of baseballs and gloves

```
P                    P

P                    P

P                    P

P                    P
```

## COACH

- Start by throwing balls to model good throws for the drill. Throws should be short-hopped balls thrown directly in front of players.
- Monitor each pair of players to make sure the proper fielding technique is being demonstrated.

## PLAYER

- Begin without gloves, using softer balls such as rag balls or tennis balls.
- Balls that are short-hopped must be received using the proper fielding technique—the elbows should be outside of the rib cage to allow the hands to be pulled toward the waist.
- Start with both hands on the ground. Begin without gloves, the hands stay on the ground, focus on the ball.
- Gradually move to the use of gloves, pair up with another player and throw the ball to each other.

# 9. Back Hand

**Primary Skill:** Backhanding a short hop

**Objective:** To develop and practice the skill of backhanding a ground ball and/or a thrown ball.

**Equipment Needed:** One baseball per pair and gloves

```
P                    P

P                    P

P                    P

P                    P
         COACH
```

## COACH

- Demonstrate the proper technique before beginning the drill.
- Circulate to each pair, emphasizing the quality of the repetitions not the quantity.

## PLAYER

- Pair up, setting up approximately 15 feet apart.
- Kneel on the knee to the side of the throwing arm, with the front side closed to your partner.
- Take turns short-hopping the ball to your partner.
- Start with your glove on the ground, keeping your wrist and your elbow loose and ready to react to the thrown ball.

# 10.  Four Corners

**Primary Skill:** Receiving and throwing

**Objective:** To develop quick feet, quick hands, glove and throwing hand relationship and the proper throwing position of arm.

**Equipment Needed:** One baseball per group and gloves

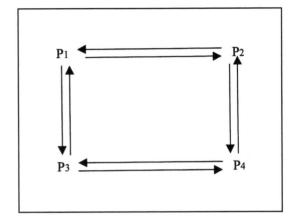

## COACH

- Monitor the drill, checking for proper technique.
- Stress quality not quantity.

## PLAYER

- Form a square with players approximately 15 yards apart.
- Start the ball in one corner, throwing to the player on the left.
- When receiving the throw, have both hands extended, elbows slightly bent, giving the thrower a target.
- As soon as the ball is caught, the feet, hands and arm quickly prepare to throw the ball to the next player.
- Continue the ball around square for five repetitions.
- After five repetitions reverse the direction of the ball; when this happens the hands and feet have to get to the throwing position quicker. The hips and feet will get the body there.
- Continue again for five repetitions or however many are needed.

# 11. Bag Coverage

**Primary Skill:** Bag coverage

**Objective:** To develop and practice the proper movement and positioning relative to the base while receiving a throw.

**Equipment Needed:** Half a dozen baseballs, baseball gloves and a throw-down base

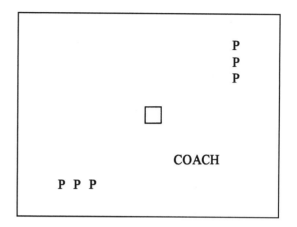

## COACH

- Position players about 10 to 15 feet in front of the bag, behind the pitcher's mound. Use cones or other markers to provide a consistent starting point.

- Give the player a signal to start moving toward the bag.

- As the player gets set at the bag, throw the ball to the bag. Vary throws, short hops, to the left or right, even throws that pull the player off the bag.

- Pay close attention to the bag position by the player; because of the closeness of the drill, work on the feet positioning and glove placement.

## PLAYER

- Align approximately 10 to 15 feet off the second base bag, half on the shortstop side while the other half is on the second baseman side.

- Break for the bag on the signal, preparing to receive the throw.

- Receive the throw in a position with the toe sweeping the front of the bag. Return the ball and then move to the end of the line.

- Initially, alternate from side to side, eventually involving both sides. One covers the bag while the other backs up.

# 12. Cut-Off

**Primary Skill:** Cut-off technique

**Objective:** To develop the proper body, hand, arm and throwing position employed during a cut-off situation.

**Equipment Needed:** One baseball per group

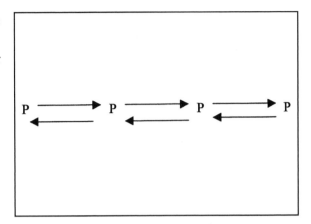

## COACH

- Monitor the technique, such as the body position, while receiving and throwing the ball.
- The cut-off technique should be taught prior to the drill.

## PLAYER

- Align approximately 15 yards apart in a straight line.
- The end man on either end of the line starts with the ball, throwing to the next player.
- When receiving the ball, get the body in the proper position: the throwing arm should be facing the thrower, the glove arm facing the next man in the line.
- When receiving the ball, reach out with both hands so the throwing arm is in better position for a quicker throw.
- Plant the throwing foot, pushing off for a quick throw; at this distance another step is probably not needed.
- Repeat this down the line and then back through in the opposite direction.
- While throwing the ball, focus on a good throw to the next player's chest or glove.

# 13. Ground Ball Mania

**Primary Skill:** Fielding ground balls

**Objective:** To practice the proper technique for fielding ground balls through maximum repetitions.

**Equipment Needed:** A bag of baseballs, a fungo bat and gloves

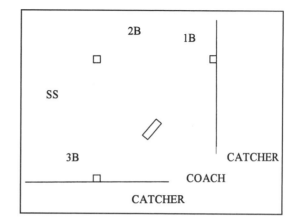

## COACH

- Set the pace for the drill, keep it moving, give the infielders maximum number of ground balls within a 5 to 10 minute time period.

- While one ball is being thrown to the catcher, another ball should be on its way to the next fielder.

- Rotate the balls around the infield, third base to first base, then first base back to third base.

- Vary the ground balls—slow, hard, high choppers, down the line, in the holes.

## PLAYER

- Align in regular positions.

- Initially start on the edge of the grass to practice a close infield technique, knock the ball down, keep it in front and then release it.

- After a few rotations move to halfway, then to a normal depth.

# 14. Fielding Bunts

**Primary Skill:** Fielding bunts

**Objective:** To practice and reinforce the proper fielding technique when fielding a bunt.

**Equipment Needed:** A bag of baseballs and gloves

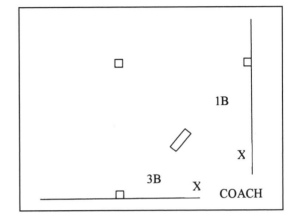

## COACH

- Set up the drill by placing the ball slightly down the first and third base lines.
- Vary the drill by having the players moving to the ball or standing over the ball.
- Start the drill without a throw to practice fielding positioning.
- Adding other infielders, as well as pitchers and catchers, can also vary the drill.

## PLAYER

- When charging the ball, start on the grass or a few feet from the ball.
- First baseman: straddle the ball, head down, field it with the hand and glove together and then step toward the target.
- Third baseman: charge, straddle, field it with the hand and glove, move toward the target while throwing.
- If the ball stops, barehand the ball, pushing it into the ground while grasping it.

# 15.  Double Play Bag Work

**Primary Skill:** Double play technique

**Objective:** To develop the proper receiving, footwork and throwing skills needed to turn a double play.

**Equipment Needed:** A dozen baseballs, base and gloves

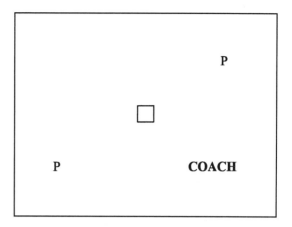

## COACH

- Initially, keep the drill at close quarters, present the ball to the second baseman or shortstop. Alternate the lines after each repetition.
- Flip the ball chest high, allowing the players to concentrate on footwork.
- Eventually widen the drill, have the shortstop and second baseman field balls, then throw to the bag. This requires increased concentration—catching a thrown ball and working on footwork at the bag.
- Take the time to teach the proper throwing technique to the shortstop and second baseman. If close to the bag, the second baseman drops to the left knee, the elbow high, squares shoulders then snaps the ball; the shortstop drops to the right knee, the elbow high, squares shoulders and snaps the ball to the bag.

## PLAYER

- Work on different steps to the bag and across the bag, preparing to throw to second base.
   —The hands should be out in front, chest high, providing a target.
   —Touch the bag with the left foot, plant the right foot, then step to throw.
   —Stay on the right field side of second.
   —Step on the bag with the left foot while crossing it and then land on the right foot to throw.
   —Drag the left foot across back of the bag, plant the right foot to throw.
- Shortstop: the hands should be out in front, chest high, providing a target.
   —Drag the right foot across the back of the bag, square shoulders and feet to make the throw.
   —Drag the right foot across the right field side of the bag, then make the throw.

# 16.  Run-Down Line

**Primary Skill:** Movement and rotation during a run-down situation

**Objective:** To practice and reinforce rotation movements used during a run-down situation.

**Equipment Needed:** One baseball per group

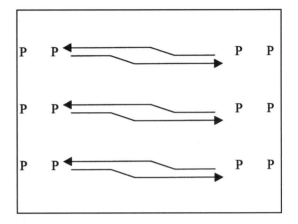

## COACH

- Set up the drill by splitting the infielders into groups of four. Split each group of four into pairs aligning approximately 20 yards apart facing each other.
- Demonstrate the proper technique by walking through rotation.
- Then start the drill with the players walking through the proper technique and rotation.

## PLAYER

- Throw or run the ball toward the next player. The proper technique should be practiced during the drill.
- Once the ball is released, continue in the same direction as the ball, getting out of the base path.
- Continue the rotation until everyone is back to his or her original position.

# 17. Fly Ball

**Primary Skill:** Catching a fly ball

**Objective:** To develop the proper movement toward the ball, body position, foot position and throwing position.

**Equipment Needed:** Baseballs and gloves

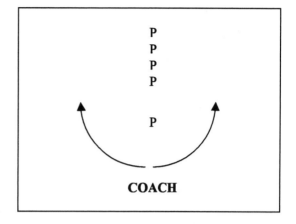

## COACH

- Position about 15 to 20 yards from the players, throwing the balls directly over the player's right shoulder, then left shoulder.

## PLAYER

- React to the coach's thrown ball either to the left or right. Use a crossover step for initial reaction.
- Turn and run to the spot, look for the ball, then position the body for throwing; glove arm should be facing the target.
- Keep the hands together while catching the ball, planting the back foot to throw.
- Catch the ball and make the throw immediately.

# 18. Line Drive

**Primary Skill:** Fielding a line drive

**Objective:** To develop movement toward the ball, the ability to field while moving and shifting the feet to throwing position after the catch.

**Equipment Needed:** Baseballs and gloves

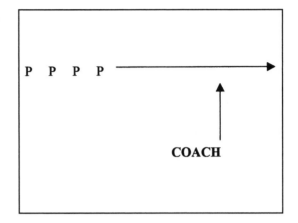

## COACH

- Position about 10 to 15 yards from the players.
- As the players jog across in front, throw the ball on a line ahead of the player.
- Gauge the throw to the speed of the player. Start with a softer throw, increasing the speed after a few repetitions.
- Make sure the players switch directions after each repetition.
- Place one player next to you to receive throws. Rotate the players at this spot.

## PLAYER

- Form a line to the left or right of the coach, approximately 10 to 15 yards away.
- Jog half speed in front of the coach.
- When the ball is thrown, concentrate on the ball as the catch is made. Extend for the ball if needed.
- Once the catch is made, gather your feet quickly to the throwing position; the body will follow.
- Make the throw when your feet are positioned properly.

# 19. Ground Ball Footwork

**Primary Skill:** Proper footwork

**Objective:** To get into position in front of the ball using the proper footwork.

**Equipment Needed:** A bag of baseballs

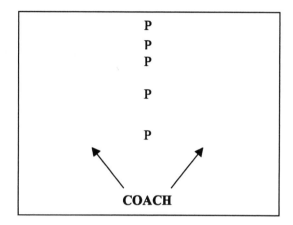

## COACH

- Demonstrate the proper technique prior to the drill.
- Put the players in a single line, bringing the first in line a few feet in front of the others.
- Start with a bag of balls; roll a ball 5 to 10 feet to the left of the first player performing the drill.
- Work through the line of players, each taking one repetition to the same side. When all the players have taken one repetition, repeat the drill in the other direction.

## PLAYER

- Get in the proper stance to field a ground ball; wait for the coach to roll a ball to the right or left.
- Once the ball is rolled, use a crossover step to help get your body in front of the ball, then allow the ball to roll between your legs.

**NOTE:** Gloves are not needed for this drill. Also, if the ball rolls directly between the player's legs, the proper position was achieved.

# 20. Bad Hops

**Primary Skill:** Fielding bad hops or bounces

**Objective:** To reinforce the proper technique for fielding bad hops or bounces.

**Equipment Needed:** One baseball per pair and gloves

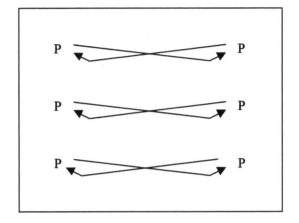

## COACH

- Demonstrate the proper fielding technique during the bad hop drill.
- Pair the infielders, making sure each pair has one baseball.
- Circulate to all pairs of infielders, critiquing technique as well as giving positive feedback.

## PLAYER

- Pair up with another infielder; face each other approximately 15 to 20 feet apart on your knees.
- Throw a bad hop directly in front of your partner. Using quick hands, an attempt is made to field the ball.
- Once the ball is fielded, a bad hop throw is returned.

# 21. Relay Throws

**Primary Skill:** Body position during relay throws

**Objective**: To reinforce and develop the proper body position used to receive and throw during a relay situation.

**Equipment Needed:** One baseball per group and gloves

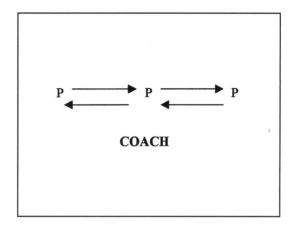

## COACH

- Demonstrate the proper body positioning while receiving the ball and throwing the ball during a relay situation.
- Place the infielders in groups of three spread out the length of the gym.
- Monitor each group, providing positive feedback during the drill.

## PLAYER

- Align in groups of three, spreading out the length of the gym.
- Start the ball on either end of the line, throwing the ball to middle. When the ball is received in the middle, use the proper body position and then open your body to throwing side to relay the ball to the other end. Once the ball is received on the other end, practice a tag.
- Start the drill over in the other direction. Repeat the drill four to five times then switch positions.

# 22. Off-Balance Throws—On the Field

**Primary Skill:** Off-balance throws

**Objective:** To practice off-balance throws to first base.

**Equipment Needed:** Bag of baseballs and gloves

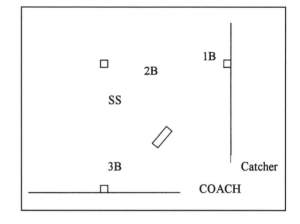

## COACH

- Align the players at infield positions; explain the purpose of the drill before starting.
- Hit or throw balls to create the need for infielders to make off-balance throws.

## PLAYER

- Align in infield positions, waiting for the balls to be hit or thrown by the coach.
- Charge the balls, fielding and throwing as quickly as possible. Try not to set first and then throw. This drill is to simulate a hurried, off-balanced throw.

# 23. Off-Balance Throws—In the Gym

**Primary Skill:** Hurried, off-balance throws

**Objective:** To practice hurried, off-balance throws.

**Equipment Needed:** Baseballs and gloves

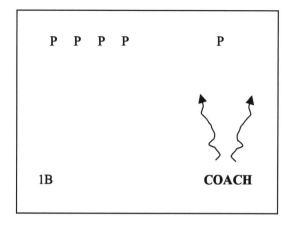

## COACH

- Align the players in a single line in the gym, with a first baseman or catcher as a receiver.

- Hit or throw balls, creating a situation requiring hurried or off-balance throws for the infielders.

## PLAYER

- Align in a single-file line at one end of the gym, having the first player in line step out in front to take a repetition.

- Charge the ball, fielding and throwing as quickly as possible. Do not try to set first then throw. This drill is to simulate a hurried, off-balance throw.

# 24. Bad Ball Drill at First Base

**Primary Skill:** Fielding bad throws at first base

**Objective:** To practice and reinforce fielding throws in the dirt.

**Equipment Needed:** A bag of baseballs, gloves and a base

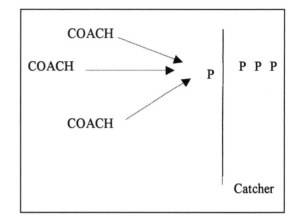

## COACH

· · · · · · · · · · · · · · · · · · · · · · · ·

- Put all first basemen at first base. One player starts at the bag to take the first repetition, while the others stand in foul territory helping with missed balls.

- Reinforce the proper technique by demonstrating it prior to the drill.

- Stand 20 to 30 feet away; throw balls in the dirt in front of the player. Throw balls from different angles: third base, shortstop and second base. Throw five balls from each direction.

## PLAYER

· · · · · · · · · · · · · · · · · · · · · · · ·

- Align at first base with one player at the bag to take the initial repetition.

- Set at first base with shoulders square to the coach and feet straddling the bag. Do not commit either foot until the ball is thrown.

- Wait for the coach's throw; commit the proper foot to bag, while reaching out with the other foot and glove. The goal is to catch the ball; if that is not possible, short hop the ball.

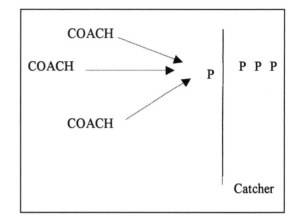

# 25. Footwork at First Base

**Primary Skill:** Proper footwork at first base

**Objective:** To practice and reinforce the proper footwork at first base.

**Equipment Needed:** A bag of baseballs, gloves and a base

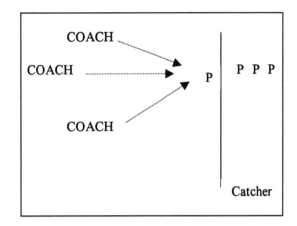

## COACH

. . . . . . . . . . . . . . . . . . . . . . . .

- Demonstrate the proper technique prior to starting the drill.

- Align the first baseman at the first base bag, having one player starting at the bag, while others are in foul territory waiting repetitions and chasing missed balls.

- Stand 20 to 30 feet away; throw balls to the player at the bag. Throw the balls from different angles: third base, shortstop and second base. Create situations so the first baseman has to use a different foot to step on the base each time. Throw five balls from each direction.

## PLAYER

. . . . . . . . . . . . . . . . . . . . . . . .

- Align at first base with one player at the bag to take the initial repetition.

- Set at first base with shoulders square to the coach and feet straddling the bag. Do not commit either foot until the ball is thrown.

- Wait for the coach's throw; commit proper foot to the bag, while reaching out with the other foot and glove.

# 26. Fly Ball Drill—Catcher and Third Baseman

**Primary Skill:** Catching fly balls and communicating

**Objective:** To improve the chance of catching fly balls down the third base line through better communication between the catcher and third baseman.

**Equipment Needed:** A bag of baseballs, gloves and a fungo bat

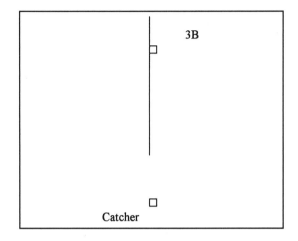

## COACH

• Discuss communication between both players prior to the drill.

• Start with the catcher and third baseman in the regular infield alignment. Hit or throw fly balls along the third base line between home and third base, involving both the catcher and third baseman.

## PLAYER

• Align in regular infield positions facing the coach. Wait for the coach to hit or throw a fly ball along the third base line between home and third.

• Once the ball is hit, move toward the ball, communicating with the catcher or third baseman, keeping the ball slightly in front of you. Make the catch with both hands above your head.

# 27. Fly Ball Drill—Shortstop and Second Baseman

**Primary Skill:** Catching fly balls and communicating

**Objective:** To improve the chance of catching fly balls in the middle infield through better communication between the shortstop and second baseman.

**Equipment Needed:** A bag of baseballs, gloves and a fungo bat

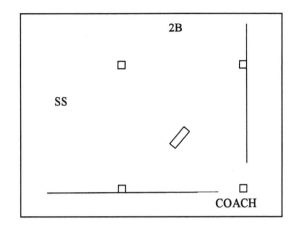

## COACH

- Discuss communication between both players prior to the drill.

- Start with the shortstop and second baseman in a regular infield alignment. Hit or throw fly balls in the middle infield, involving both the shortstop and second baseman.

## PLAYER

- Align in regular infield positions facing the coach. Wait for the coach to hit or throw a fly ball in the middle infield.

- Once the ball is hit, move toward the ball, communicating with the shortstop or second baseman, keeping the ball slightly in front of you. Make the catch with both hands above your head.

# 28. Fly Ball Drill—Shortstop and Third Baseman

**Primary Skill:** Catching fly balls and communicating

**Objective:** To improve the chance of catching fly balls down the third base line through better communication between the shortstop and third baseman.

**Equipment Needed:** A bag of baseballs, gloves and a fungo bat

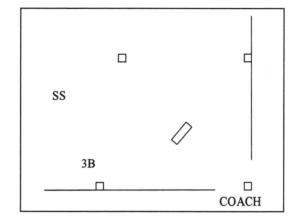

## COACH

• Discuss communication between both players prior to the drill.

• Start with the shortstop and third baseman in regular infield alignment. Hit or throw fly balls down the third base line, involving both the shortstop and third baseman.

## PLAYER

• Align in regular infield positions facing the coach. Wait for the coach to hit or throw a fly ball down the third base line.

• Once the ball is hit, move toward the ball, communicating with the shortstop or third baseman, keeping the ball slightly in front of you. Make the catch with both hands above your head.

# 29. Fly Ball Drill—First Baseman and Second Baseman

**Primary Skill:** Catching fly balls and communicating

**Objective:** To improve the chance of catching fly balls down first base line through better communication between the first baseman and second baseman.

**Equipment Needed:** A bag of baseballs, gloves and a fungo bat

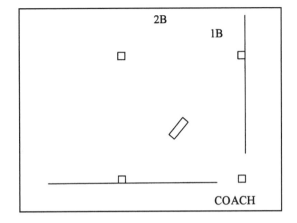

## COACH

- Discuss communication between both players prior to the drill.

- Start with the first baseman and second baseman in regular infield alignment. Hit or throw fly balls down the first base line, involving both the first baseman and second baseman.

## PLAYER

- Align in regular infield positions facing the coach. Wait for the coach to hit or throw a fly ball down the first base line.

- Once the ball is hit, move toward the ball, communicating with the first baseman or second baseman, keeping the ball slightly in front of you. Make the catch with both hands above your head.

# 30. Fly Ball Drill—Catcher and First Baseman

**Primary Skill:** Catching fly balls and communicating

**Objective:** To improve catching fly balls down first base line through better communication between the catcher and first baseman.

**Equipment Needed:** A bag of baseballs, gloves and a fungo bat

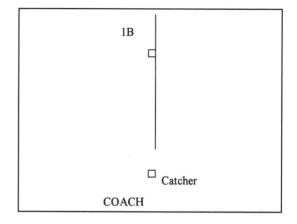

## COACH

- Discuss communication between both players prior to the drill.
- Start with the catcher and first baseman in regular infield alignment. Hit or throw fly balls down the first base line between home and first base, involving both the catcher and first baseman.

## PLAYER

- Align in regular infield positions facing the coach. Wait for the coach to hit or throw a fly ball down the first base line between home and first base.
- Once the ball is hit, move toward the ball, communicating with the first baseman or catcher, keeping the ball slightly in front of you. Make the catch with both hands above your head.

# 31. Holding Runner Close—First Base

**Primary Skill:** Holding runner close to first base

**Objective:** To improve and reinforce techniques for holding the runner close to first base.

**Equipment Needed:** Six baseballs, gloves and a base

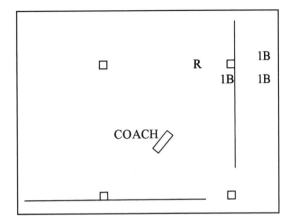

## COACH

- Place the first baseman at first base, having one player starting at the bag to take initial repetitions. Talk through and demonstrate the proper alignment as well as the proper technique to tag the runner prior to the drill.

- Use other players as runners with leads at first base; others can help with missed balls.

- Stand 20 feet away from the base, mimicking the pitcher's motion. Initially, make throws to first base every repetition. Throws should be good and bad, forcing the players to react to bad throws.

- As the drill progresses, alternate the throws to first base and movement to home as well.

## PLAYER

- Align at first base with one player taking the initial repetition; others become the runners and backups for missed balls.

- Take the proper position holding the runner at first base, watching the throw from the coach. After receiving the throw, place the tag on the runner attempting to get back to the bag.

- If the coach makes a movement toward home with the ball, get off the bag, ready to field the position.

# 32. Holding Runner Close—Second Base

**Primary Skill:** Holding runner close to second base

**Objective:** To improve and reinforce techniques for holding the runner close to second base.

**Equipment Needed:** Six baseballs, gloves and a base

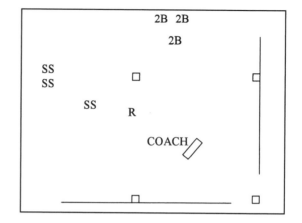

## COACH

- Place the shortstop and second baseman in regular infield positions, having two players starting at these positions to take the initial repetitions. Talk through and demonstrate the proper alignment.

- Use other players as the runners leading off second base; others can help with missed balls.

- Stand 20 feet away from the base, mimicking the pitcher's motion. Initially, make throws to second base every repetition. Throws should be good and bad, forcing the players to react to bad throws.

- As the drill progresses, alternate the throws to second base and movement to home as well.

## PLAYER

- Align at shortstop and second base with one player taking the initial repetition at each position; others become the runners and backups for missed balls.

- Take the proper position holding the runner at second base; coordinate movement between the shortstop and second baseman, watching for the throw from the coach. After receiving the throw, place the tag on the runner attempting to get back to the bag. If the coach makes a movement toward home with the ball, get back to your original positions, ready to field.

© 2001 by Prentice Hall

# 33. Holding Runner Close—Third Base

**Primary Skill:** Holding runner close to third base

**Objective:** To improve and reinforce techniques for holding the runner close to third base.

**Equipment Needed:** Six baseballs, gloves and a base

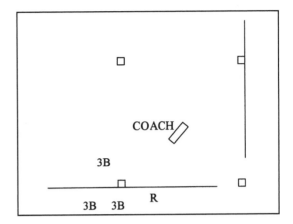

## COACH

• Place the third baseman in regular infield position, having one player starting at third base to take initial repetitions. Talk through and demonstrate the proper alignment.

• Use other players as the runners leading off third base; others can help with missed balls.

• Stand 20 feet away from base, mimicking the pitcher's motion. Initially, make throws to third base every repetition. Throws should be good and bad, forcing players to react to bad throws.

• As the drill progresses, alternate the throws to third base and movement to home as well.

## PLAYER

• Align at third base with one player taking the initial repetition, while others become the runners and backups for missed balls.

• Take the proper position holding the runner at third base, watching for the throw from the coach. After receiving the throw, place the tag on the runner attempting to get back to the bag. If the coach makes a movement toward home with the ball, get back to your original positions, ready to field.

# 34. Double Play Pivot—Shortstop

**Primary Skill:** Shortstop double play technique

**Objective:** To practice proper approach and footwork for the shortstop turning a double play.

**Equipment Needed:** Six baseballs, gloves and a base

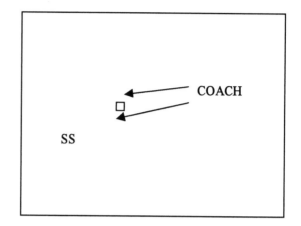

## COACH

- Talk through shortstop pivots prior to the drill.
- Place the shortstops at a normal infield position or in the gym with a throw-down bag at an approximate distance.
- Stand 15 to 20 feet from the bag, giving the shortstop three different looks: a throw from the second baseman, from the first baseman and a ground ball close to the bag.

## PLAYER

- Align in a normal shortstop position or an approximate distance from the bag in the gym.
- Wait for the coach's signal to approach the bag; the type of approach will be determined by the angle of the throw. On a throw from the second baseman, drag the foot to the right field side of the bag; on a throw from the first baseman, drag the foot on the inside of second base; on a ground ball near the bag, the shortstop takes the ball.

# 35. Double Play Pivot—Second Base

**Primary Skill:** Second baseman double play technique

**Objective:** To practice proper approach and footwork for the second baseman turning a double play.

**Equipment Needed:** Six baseballs, gloves and a base

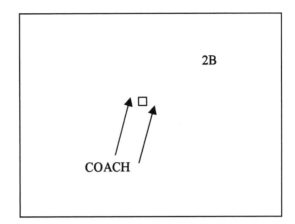

## COACH

- Discuss aspects of the second baseman pivot prior to the drill.
- Place the second baseman at a normal infield position or in the gym with a throw-down bag at an approximate distance.
- Stand 15 to 20 feet from the bag, giving the second baseman three different looks: a throw from the shortstop, from the third baseman and a ground ball close to the bag.

## PLAYER

- Align in a normal second base position or an approximate distance from the bag in the gym.
- Wait for the coach's signal to approach the bag; the type of approach will be determined by the angle of the throw. For a throw from the shortstop or third baseman, step on the bag with the left foot or touch the right field side of the bag; for a ground ball near the bag, the second baseman takes the ball.

# 36. Backhand Toss—Second Base

**Primary Skill:** Backhand toss

**Objective:** To develop and practice the backhand toss by the second baseman to the shortstop covering second base.

**Equipment Needed:** Six baseballs, gloves and a base

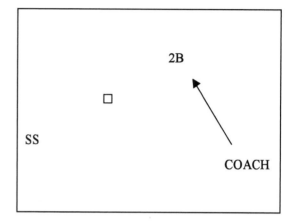

## COACH

- Demonstrate the technique prior to the start of the drill.
- Place the second baseman at a position approximately 10 to 15 feet from the second base bag. Place the shortstop in a regular double play position to take tosses at the bag.
- Stand behind the pitcher's mound with baseballs, give the players a ready signal and then roll one ball to the player taking the repetition.
- Provide constant suggestions for improvement, as well as encouragement.
- Work through the drill as many times as needed.

## PLAYER

- Align at a second base position, approximately 10 to 15 feet from second base, while the shortstop aligns at a double play position. Step forward to take repetitions.
- Both players get into a ready position when the coach gives a ready signal prior to throwing the ball.
- Once the ball is rolled, move toward the ball, first fielding the ball properly, then backhand toss the ball to the shortstop covering the bag at second base. Take a repetition, then move to the back of the line.

# 37. Underhand Toss—Second Base

**Primary Skill:** Underhand toss

**Objective:** To develop and practice the underhand toss by the second baseman to the shortstop covering second base.

**Equipment Needed:** Six baseballs, gloves and a base

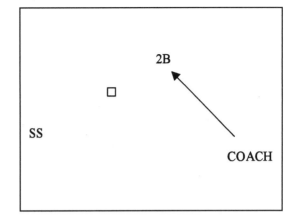

## COACH

- Demonstrate the technique prior to start of the drill.

- Place the second baseman at a position approximately 10 to 15 feet from the bag. Place the shortstop in a regular double play position to take tosses at second base.

- Stand behind the pitcher's mound with baseballs, give the players a ready signal and then roll one ball to the player taking the repetition.

- Provide constant suggestions for improvement, as well as encouragement.

- Work through the drill as many times as needed.

## PLAYER

- Align at a second base position, approximately 10 to 15 feet from second base, while the shortstop aligns at a double play position. Step forward to take repetitions.

- Both players get into a ready position when the coach gives a ready signal prior to throwing the ball.

- Once the ball is rolled, move toward the ball, first fielding the ball properly, then underhand toss the ball to the shortstop covering the bag at second base. Take repetition, then move to the back of the line.

# 38. Jump-Pivot Toss—Second Base

**Primary Skill:** Jump-pivot toss

**Objective:** To develop and practice the jump-pivot toss by the second baseman to the shortstop covering second base.

**Equipment Needed:** Six baseballs, gloves and a base

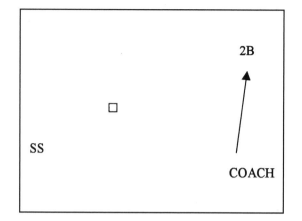

## COACH

- Demonstrate the technique prior to start of the drill.

- Place the second baseman at a regular second base position. Place the shortstop in a regular double play position to take tosses at the bag.

- Stand behind the pitcher's mound with baseballs, give the players a ready signal and then roll one ball to the player taking the repetition.

- Provide constant suggestions for improvement as well as encouragement.

- Work through the drill as many times as needed.

## PLAYER

- Align at a regular second base position, while the shortstop aligns at a double-play position. Step forward to take repetitions.

- Both players get into a ready position when the coach gives a ready signal prior to throwing the ball.

- Once the ball is rolled, move toward the ball, first fielding the ball properly, then jump-pivot toss the ball to shortstop covering the bag. Take repetition, then move to the back of the line.

# 39. One-Knee Toss—Second Base

**Primary Skill:** One-knee toss

**Objective:** To develop and practice the one-knee toss by the second baseman to the shortstop covering the second base.

**Equipment Needed:** Six baseballs, gloves and a base

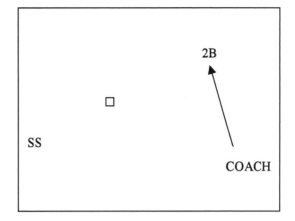

## COACH

· · · · · · · · · · · · · · · · · · · · · · ·

- Demonstrate the technique prior to start of the drill.

- Place the second baseman at a position approximately 20 to 25 feet from the bag. Place the shortstop in a regular double play position to take tosses at second base.

- Stand behind the pitcher's mound with baseballs, give the players a ready signal and then roll one ball to the player taking the repetition.

- Provide constant suggestions for improvement as well as encouragement.

- Work through the drill as many times as needed.

## PLAYER

· · · · · · · · · · · · · · · · · · · · · · ·

- Align at the second base position, approximately 20 to 25 feet from second base, while the shortstop aligns at a double play position. Step forward to take repetitions.

- Both players get into a ready position when the coach gives a ready signal prior to throwing the ball.

- Once the ball is rolled, move toward the ball, first fielding the ball properly, then one-knee toss the ball to the shortstop covering the bag at second base. Take repetition, then move to the back of the line.

# 40. Toss Combo Drill—Second Base

**Primary Skill:** Tosses to second base

**Objective:** To develop and practice the different tosses used by the second baseman to the shortstop covering second base.

**Equipment Needed:** Six baseballs, gloves and a base

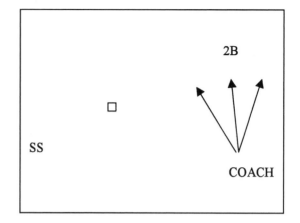

## COACH

- Demonstrate the technique prior to start of the drill.
- Place the second baseman at regular position. Place the shortstop in a regular double play position to take tosses at the base.
- Stand behind the pitcher's mound with baseballs, give the players a ready signal and then roll balls at different angles to provide the player opportunities for making different tosses.
- Provide constant suggestions for improvement as well as encouragement.
- Work through the drill as many times as needed.

## PLAYER

- Align at second base in a regular position, while shortstop aligns at a double play position. Step forward to take repetitions.
- Both players get into a ready position when the coach gives a ready signal prior to throwing the ball.
- Once the ball is rolled, move toward the ball, first fielding the ball properly and then use an appropriate toss to the shortstop covering second base. Take repetition, then move to the back of the line.

# 41. Backhand Toss—Shortstop

**Primary Skill:** Backhand toss

**Objective:** To develop and practice the backhand toss by the shortstop to the second baseman covering the base.

**Equipment Needed:** Six baseballs, gloves and a base

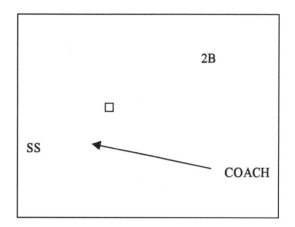

## COACH

- Demonstrate the technique prior to start of the drill.

- Place the shortstop at a position approximately 10 to 15 feet from second base. Place the second baseman in a regular double play position to take tosses at the bag.

- Stand behind the pitcher's mound with baseballs, give the players a ready signal and then roll one ball to the player taking the repetition.

- Provide constant suggestions for improvement as well as encouragement.

- Work through the drill as many times as needed.

## PLAYER

- Align at the shortstop position, approximately 10 to 15 feet from second base, while the second baseman aligns at a double play position. Step forward to take repetitions.

- Both players get into a ready position when the coach gives a ready signal prior to throwing the ball.

- Once the ball is rolled, move toward the ball, first fielding the ball properly, then backhand toss the ball to the second baseman covering the bag at second base. Take repetition, then move to the back of the line.

# 42. Underhand Toss—Shortstop

**Primary Skill:** Underhand toss

**Objective:** To develop and practice the underhand toss by the shortstop to the second baseman covering the base.

**Equipment Needed:** Six baseballs, gloves and a base

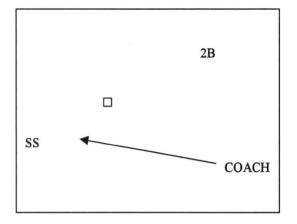

## COACH

- Demonstrate the technique prior to start of the drill.
- Place the shortstop at a position approximately 10 to 15 feet from second base. Place the second baseman in a regular double play position to take tosses at the bag.
- Stand behind the pitcher's mound with baseballs, give the players a ready signal and then roll one ball to the player taking the repetition.
- Provide constant suggestions for improvement as well as encouragement.
- Work through the drill as many times as needed.

## PLAYER

- Align at the shortstop position, approximately 10 to 15 feet from second base, while the second baseman aligns at a double play position. Step forward to take repetitions.
- Both players get into a ready position when the coach gives a ready signal prior to throwing the ball.
- Once the ball is rolled, move toward the ball, first fielding the ball properly, then underhand toss the ball to the second baseman covering the bag at second base. Take repetition, then move to the back of the line.

# 43. One-Knee Toss—Shortstop

**Primary Skill:** One-knee toss

**Objective:** To develop and practice the one-knee toss by the shortstop to the second baseman covering the base.

**Equipment Needed:** Six baseballs, gloves and a base

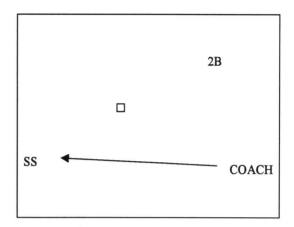

## COACH

- Demonstrate the technique prior to start of the drill.

- Place the shortstop at a position approximately 20 to 25 feet from second base. Place the second baseman in a regular double play position to take tosses at the bag.

- Stand behind the pitcher's mound with baseballs, give the players a ready signal and then roll one ball to the player taking the repetition.

- Provide constant suggestions for improvement as well as encouragement.

- Work through the drill as many times as needed.

## PLAYER

- Align at the shortstop position, approximately 20 to 25 feet from second base, while the second baseman aligns at a double play position. Step forward to take repetitions.

- Both players get into a ready position when the coach gives a ready signal prior to throwing the ball.

- Once the ball is rolled, move toward the ball, first fielding the ball properly, then one-knee toss the ball to the second baseman covering the bag at second base. Take repetition, then move to the back of the line.

# 44. Sidearm Toss—Shortstop

**Primary Skill:** Sidearm toss

**Objective:** To develop and practice the sidearm toss by the shortstop to the second baseman covering the base.

**Equipment Needed:** Six baseballs, gloves and a base

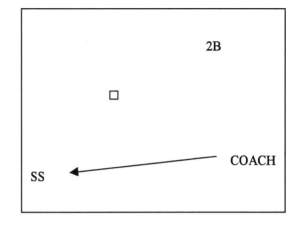

## COACH

- Demonstrate the technique prior to start of the drill.
- Place the shortstop at a regular position. Place the second baseman in a regular double play position to take tosses at second base.
- Stand behind the pitcher's mound with baseballs, give the players a ready signal and then roll one ball to the player taking the repetition.
- Provide constant suggestions for improvement as well as encouragement.
- Work through the drill as many times as needed.

## PLAYER

- Align at a regular shortstop position, while the second baseman aligns at a double play position. Step forward to take repetitions.
- Both players get into a ready position when the coach gives a ready signal prior to throwing the ball.
- Once the ball is rolled, move toward the ball, first fielding the ball properly, then sidearm toss the ball to the second baseman covering the bag. Take repetition, then move to the back of the line.

# 45. Toss Combo Drill—Shortstop

**Primary Skill:** Tosses to second base

**Objective:** To develop and practice the different tosses used by the shortstop to throw to the second baseman covering the base.

**Equipment Needed:** Six baseballs, gloves and a base

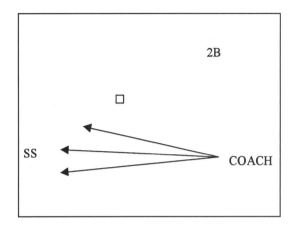

## COACH

- Demonstrate the technique prior to start of the drill.

- Place the shortstop at a regular position. Place the second baseman in a regular double play position to take tosses at the bag.

- Stand behind the pitcher's mound with baseballs, give the players a ready signal and then roll the balls at different angles to provide the player opportunities for making different tosses.

- Provide constant suggestions for improvement as well as encouragement.

- Work through the drill as many times as needed.

## PLAYER

- Align at shortstop in a regular position, while the second baseman aligns at a double play position. Step forward to take repetitions.

- Both players get into a ready position when the coach gives a ready signal prior to throwing the ball.

- Once the ball is rolled, move toward the ball, first fielding the ball properly, and then use the appropriate toss to the second baseman covering the bag. Take repetition, then move to the back of the line.

# 46. Taking Throws at Second Base

**Primary Skill:** Receiving throws at the bag

**Objective:** To practice moving toward the second base and receiving a throw from the catcher.

**Equipment Needed:** Six baseballs, gloves and a base

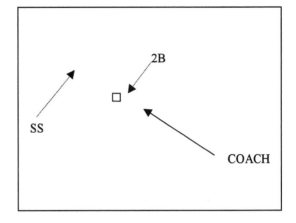

## COACH

- Demonstrate the proper technique and movement prior to the drill.

- Align the second basemen and shortstops in normal positioning when covering the bag. One player at each position steps forward to take the repetition.

- Stand behind the pitcher's mound to control the drill. Give the players a ready signal first and then signal to move to the bag. Throw the ball when the players are almost at the bag. Vary throws so the second baseman and shortstop have to react to different situations. One covers the bag, while the other backs up the throw.

- Switch the responsibilities of the second baseman and the shortstop each time through the drill.

## PLAYER

- Align in normal positions when covering second base. Step forward to take repetitions at each position.

- Get into a good ready position; when the coach gives a signal, break to the bag for the throw. One player covers the bag, while the other backs up the throw.

- Switch responsibilities next time through the drill.

- Return the ball to the coach and then move to the back of the line.

# 47. Taking Throws at Third Base

**Primary Skill:** Receiving throws at the bag

**Objective:** To practice moving toward third base and receiving throws from the catcher.

**Equipment Needed:** Six baseballs, gloves and a base

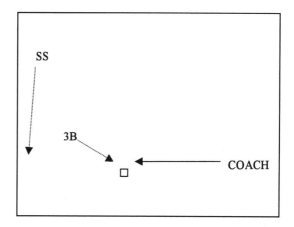

## COACH

- Demonstrate the proper technique prior to the drill.

- Align the third basemen and shortstops in normal positioning when covering the bag. One player at each position steps forward to take the repetition.

- Stand approximately halfway between third and home to throw the balls to better control the drill. Give the players a ready signal first and then signal to move to the bag. Throw the ball when the players are almost at the bag. Vary throws so the third baseman and shortstop have to react to different situations. The third baseman covers the bag, while the shortstop backs up the throw.

- Work through the drill as many times as needed.

## PLAYER

- Align in normal positions when covering the third base bag. Step forward to take repetitions at each position.

- Get into a good ready position; when the coach gives a signal, break to third base for the throw. The third baseman covers the bag, while the shortstop backs up the throw.

- Return the ball to the coach and then move to the back of the line.

# 48. Third Baseman Making Throws to Second Base

**Primary Skill:** Making throws to second base

**Objective:** To practice and reinforce the third baseman making throws to second base.

**Equipment Needed:** Six baseballs, gloves, a fungo bat and a base

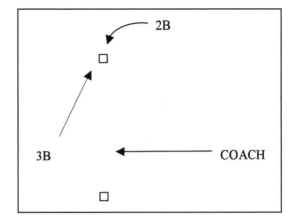

## COACH

• Place the third basemen and second basemen in regular alignments, stepping forward to take the repetition. Give a signal before throwing or hitting the ground ball to the players. If throwing, stand halfway between third and home; if hitting, stand at home plate.

• Hit a ground ball to the third baseman; once the ball is fielded it is thrown to the second baseman covering second base. The second baseman then returns the ball to the coach.

• Continue to encourage the proper fielding techniques, as well as the proper throwing techniques.

## PLAYER

• Align at normal third base and shortstop positions, stepping forward to take repetitions. As the coach is starting to throw or hit the ball, get into a good ready position.

• Once the ball is on the ground, attack the ball with the proper fielding technique and then make a good chest-high throw to the second baseman.

• The second baseman returns the ball to the coach, and then both players move to the back of the line.

# 49. First Baseman Making Throws to Second Base

**Primary Skill:** Making throws to second base bag

**Objective:** To practice and reinforce the first baseman making throws to second base.

**Equipment Needed:** Six baseballs, gloves, a fungo bat and a base

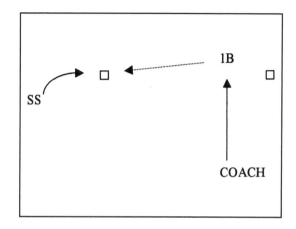

## COACH

- Place the first baseman and second baseman in regular alignment, stepping forward to take the repetition. Give a signal before throwing or hitting the ground ball to the players. If throwing, stand halfway between first and home; if hitting, stand at home plate.

- Hit a ground ball to the first baseman; once the ball is fielded it is thrown to the second baseman. The second baseman then returns the ball to the coach.

- Continue to encourage the proper fielding techniques, as well as the proper throwing techniques.

## PLAYER

- Align at normal first base and shortstop positions, stepping forward to take repetitions. As the coach is starting to throw or hit the ball, get into a good ready position.

- Once the ball is on the ground, attack the ball with the proper fielding technique and then make a good chest-high throw to the second baseman.

- The second baseman returns the ball to the coach, and then both players move to the back of the line.

# 50. Classroom Drill—Ready Position

**Primary Skill:** Proper ready position

**Objective:** To reinforce the proper ready position before and during pitch delivery.

**Equipment Needed:** None

## COACH

- Demonstrate the proper ready position and when to get into position prior to the start of the drill.

- Clear a space by moving desks to the side. Have two to three players stand side by side about an arm's length away.

- Give the players a ready signal by imitating a pitcher's movement, either a windup or stretch motion. The players should get into the ready position as soon as the motion begins.

- Critique the stance and the timing of movement to the ready position. Continue to encourage the players throughout the drill.

## PLAYER

- Step forward with two other players to take repetitions in the cleared area of the classroom. Align an arm's length away from the player to the left or right.

- Watch for the coach's movement from the windup or the stretch, get into the ready position when the movement starts.

- Take the number of repetitions as indicated by the coach before switching.

# 51. Classroom Drill—Fielding Position

**Primary Skill:** Proper fielding position

**Objective:** To reinforce the proper fielding position while attacking a ground ball.

**Equipment Needed:** None

## COACH

• Demonstrate the proper fielding position and when to get into position prior to the start of the drill.

• Clear a space by moving desks to the side. Have two to three players stand side by side about an arm's length away.

• Give the players a ready signal by imitating a pitcher's movement, either a windup or stretch motion. The players should go from the ready position as soon as the motion begins to the fielding position.

• Critique the stance and the timing of the movement to the fielding position. Continue to encourage the players throughout the drill.

## PLAYER

• Step forward with two other players to take repetitions in the cleared area of the classroom. Align an arm's length away from the player to the left or right.

• Watch for the coach's movement from the windup or the stretch; go from the ready position when the movement starts to the proper fielding position.

• Take the number of repetitions as indicated by the coach before switching.

# 52. Classroom Drill—Initial Steps

**Primary Skill:** Initial steps to ball

**Objective:** To practice the initial step when attacking a ground ball in the infield.

**Equipment Needed:** None

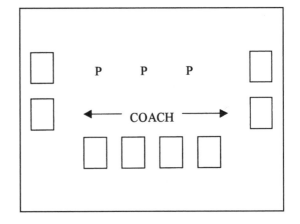

## COACH

- Demonstrate the initial steps prior to the start of the drill.
- Clear a space by moving desks to the side. Have two to three players stand side by side about an arm's length away.
- Give the players a ready signal and then give the players a hand direction either left or right to take the initial crossover step. Everything starts with the players getting into the ready position as soon as the motion begins.
- Critique stance, the timing of the movement to the ready position and the initial crossover step. Continue to encourage the players throughout the drill.

## PLAYER

- Step forward with two other players to take repetitions in the cleared area of the classroom. Align an arm's length away from the player to the left or right.
- Watch for the coach's movement from the windup or the stretch, get into the ready position when the movement starts and then watch for direction from the coach to take the initial crossover step.
- Take the number of repetitions as indicated by the coach before switching.

# 53. Charging the Ball

**Primary Skill:** Charging the ball

**Objective:** To practice charging a ground ball, reading the hop of the ball and playing through the ball.

**Equipment Needed:** Six baseballs, a fungo bat and gloves

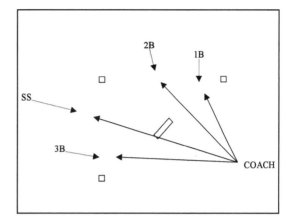

## COACH

- Talk through the purpose of the drill before the start.

- Align the infielders at one infield position approximately 20 to 25 feet behind the regular position. The player taking the repetition runs toward the regular position, so the player is moving when the ball is hit.

- Go through the line of infielders as many times as necessary.

## PLAYER

- Align at one infield position approximately 20 to 25 feet behind the regular position.

- Start running toward the regular position; watch for the coach hitting the ball. When the ball is hit, read the hop and get in a good balance position to play through the ball.

- Field the ball on the run, gathering the feet to make a good throw. Return to the back of the line after each repetition.

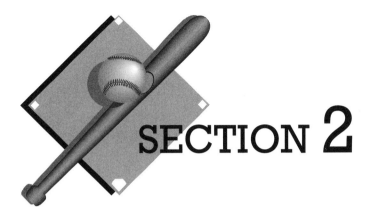

# SECTION 2

# OUTFIELD

*The quality of a person's life is in direct proportion to their commitment to excellence.*

—VINCE LOMBARDI

# 54. Long Toss

**Primary Skill:** Throwing technique, arm strengthening

**Objective:** To practice the proper throwing technique while strengthening the arm muscles.

**Equipment Needed:** One baseball per pair

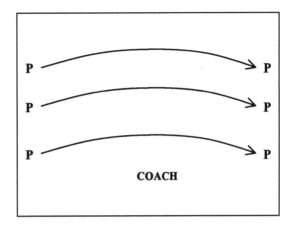

## COAGH

- Have the players pair up and face each other.
- Have them stand about 20 yards apart.
- After they begin throwing, ask them to slowly move apart.
- Watch carefully and make corrections as needed.
- Keep the pace moving. Offer continuous encouragement.

## PLAYER

- Pair up with another outfielder, starting 20 yards apart.
- Use the proper throwing and receiving techniques.
- Make a few throws at each distance, slowly moving farther apart. The goal is to be 40 to 50 yards apart.
- Receive the ball, then crow hop to throw the ball. Throw the ball with a slight arch, being careful not to overthrow, which could injure the arm.

**NOTE:** While this drill can be used for other positions, it is a good drill to use for the pitchers and catchers during pregame warm-ups. It helps to stretch muscles in the throwing arm. Take caution not to overthrow.

# 55. Proper Fielding

**Primary Skill:** Fielding

**Objective:** To develop and reinforce proper fielding of ground balls and fly balls by outfielders.

**Equipment Needed:** Six baseballs

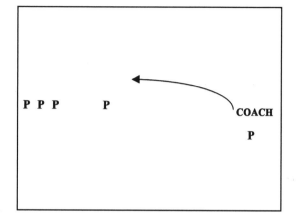

## COACH

- Demonstrate the proper technique to the players before starting the drill.
- Initially throw the balls; this provides more control to the drill.

## PLAYER

- Form a single line facing the coach. The first in line steps out in front to take the repetitions.
- One player stays with the coach to take the throws from the outfielders.
- Execute the repetition using the proper fielding technique.

**NOTE:** Adapt this drill to working solely on the fly ball technique. This is a great drill for indoor practices with the outfielders; the coach can flip the balls.

# 56. Crow Hop

**Primary Skill:** Crow hop

**Objective:** To develop and practice the crow hop for gaining momentum at the beginning of the throwing motion.

**Equipment Needed:** One baseball per pair

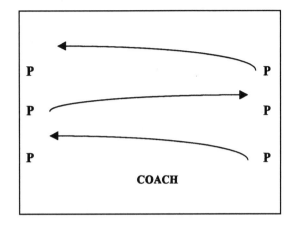

## COACH

- Demonstrate the proper crow hop technique. Show the players how the crow hop provides forward momentum while making a throw.
- Have the players pair up and face each other standing about 20 yards apart, continuing to create distance.
- Watch carefully and make corrections as needed.
- Keep the pace moving, offering continuous encouragement.

## PLAYER

- Pair up with another outfielder.
- Practice the crow hop technique while throwing to partner.
- Keep the throws to the glove side of partner.

**NOTE:** Use this technique in conjunction with other drills, such as the warm-up and long toss drill.

# 57. Throwing to the Cut-Off Man

**Primary Skill:** Cut-off throws

**Objective:** To practice and reinforce the technique of throwing the fielded ball to the cut-off man.

**Equipment Needed:** Six baseballs, a fungo bat and gloves

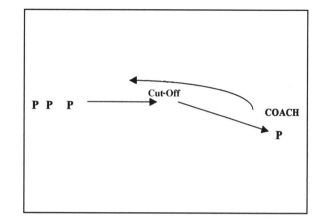

## COACH

- Set the cut-off man approximately halfway.

- Throw the balls initially to help focus on the cut-off throws, then progress to hitting the balls with a fungo.

- Keep one player to receive the throws from the cut-off man.

## PLAYER

- Step out in front to take repetitions, executing repetitions using the proper technique.

- One player stays next to the coach to take the throws from the cut-off.

- Field the ball, then crow hop to throw the ball to the cut-off.

**NOTE:** Adapt this drill to other drills by adding a cut-off man.

# 58. Fly Ball Communication

**Primary Skills:** Communication

**Objective:** To reinforce the proper communication between outfielders while fielding a fly ball.

**Equipment Needed:** Six baseballs and gloves

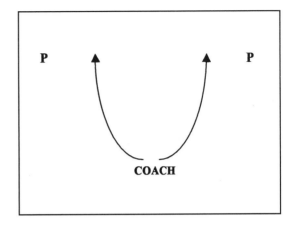

## COACH

- Demonstrate the proper communication prior to the start of the drill.

- Set up the drill with two outfielders side by side approximately 20 yards apart. Hit or throw a fly ball between the outfielders, causing them to communicate as to who will catch the ball.

## PLAYER

- Pair up with another outfielder, aligning 20 yards apart.

- Once the ball is hit, move toward the ball while communicating with the other outfielder.

- Catch the ball; gather feet to make a throw to the cut-off man.

# 59. Gap Ball

**Primary Skill:** Fielding balls in the gap

**Objective:** To practice and reinforce the fielding technique needed to approach a ball in the gap.

**Equipment Needed:** Six baseballs, a fungo bat and baseball gloves

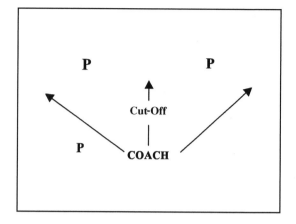

## COACH

- First demonstrate the proper footsteps and angle to the ball.
- Start with a single outfielder, eventually progressing to two. Communication is important with two outfielders.
- Initially throw the balls from a closer distance, providing more control to the drill. Progress to hitting the balls with a fungo bat. If the drill is held in the gym, throwing the balls is necessary.
- Throw the ball to either side of the outfielder—throw ground balls, line drives or fly balls.
- Use one player to receive the throws back to the coach, as well as a cut-off man when hitting the balls from a farther distance.

## PLAYER

- Step out in front to take repetition.
- Execute repetitions using the proper steps, angle to the ball and crow hop when throwing the ball.
- Field the ball and gather feet to throw the ball to the cut-off man or the catcher standing beside the coach.
- When performing the drill with two outfielders, communicate with each other. One takes the ball, the other goes to the back-up position.

**NOTE:** Adapt this drill to working solely on fly ball technique. This is a great drill for indoor practices with the outfielders since not a lot of space is needed.

# 60. Deep Ball

**Primary Skill:** Catching fly balls

**Objective:** To practice running down and catching balls hit deep, whether in the gap or directly overhead.

**Equipment Needed:** Six baseballs, gloves and a fungo bat

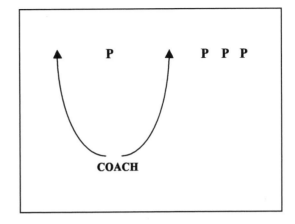

## COACH

- Demonstrate the proper technique prior to the start of the drill.
- Throw fly balls to either side or directly overhead.
- Set one player to catch the throws back to the coach.

## PLAYER

- Step out in front to take repetitions, field the ball and gather feet to throw the ball.
- One other player stands with the coach to take throws from the outfielders.
- Execute the repetitions using the proper steps.

**NOTE:** Adapt this drill to working solely on fly ball technique. This is a great drill for indoor practices with outfielders since not a lot of space is needed.

# 61. Playing the Sun

**Primary Skill:** Catching fly balls in the sun's path

**Objective:** To practice the technique of catching fly balls that require the fielder to look directly into the sun.

**Equipment Needed:** One baseball per pair and gloves

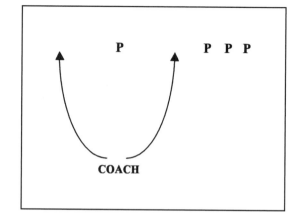

## COACH

• Demonstrate the proper technique prior to the start of the drill.

• Pair outfielders, aligning them approximately 20 yards a part. Position them so they look into the sun if possible.

• One outfielder throws a fly ball directly into the sun; the other player uses the proper technique to catch the ball.

• Work the drill about 10 to 15 repetitions.

## PLAYER

• Pair up with another outfielder, aligning 20 yards apart, with one baseball.

• Throw a fly ball to your partner either underhand or overhand; make sure your partner uses the proper technique to shield the sun while catching the ball.

• Once the catch is made, return a fly ball to your partner.

# 62. Charge—Scoop Drill

**Primary Skill:** Charging and scooping the ball

**Objective:** To practice charging and scooping a ball hit to the outfield.

**Equipment Needed:** Six baseballs, gloves and a fungo bat

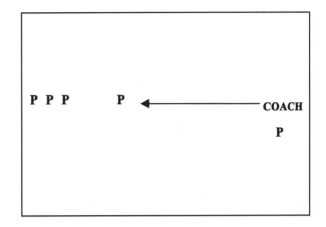

## COACH

- Set players in a single line 30 yards away, with one player in front to take initial repetition.
- Initially throw a ground ball for players to practice this technique, then move to hitting balls with a fungo bat.
- Continue to provide encouragement during the drill.

## PLAYER

- Align in a single line 30 yards from the coach. Step out in front to take repetitions.
- When the ball is thrown or hit by the coach, charge the ball aggressively, getting your body under control when nearing the ball.
- Maintain the proper stride, reach down and scoop the ball with your glove. Stride through to the throwing position.

# 63. Charge, Scoop and Throw

**Primary Skill:** Charging, scooping and throwing the ball

**Objective:** To practice charging, scooping and throwing the ball to prevent runners from taking extra bases.

**Equipment Needed:** Six baseballs, gloves and a fungo bat

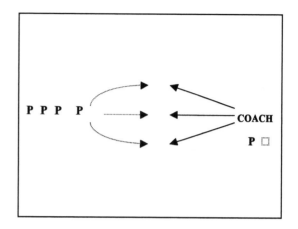

## COACH

- Set the players in a single line 30 yards away, with one player in front to take the initial repetition.

- Initially throw a ground ball for players to practice this technique, then move to hitting balls with a fungo bat. Vary the throws, from directly at a fielder to throws at either side.

- Keep one player to receive throws from the outfielders either at a base or in a cut-off position.

- Continue to provide encouragement during the drill.

## PLAYER

- Align in a single line 30 yards from the coach. Step out in front to take repetitions.

- When the ball is thrown or hit by the coach, charge the ball aggressively, circling the ball to end up facing not only the ball but also the base you intend to throw toward, getting the body under control when nearing the ball.

- Maintain the proper stride, reach down and scoop ball with the glove. Stride through to the throwing position.

# 64. Playing the Fence

**Primary Skill:** Catching fly balls and communication

**Objective:** To practice catching fly balls and developing communication while playing balls hit near the fence.

**Equipment Needed:** Six baseballs, gloves, a fungo bat and a fence or screen

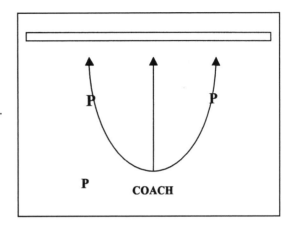

## COACH

- Talk through the technique and communication prior to the drill.
- Start with two outfielders taking repetitions 20 to 30 yards apart and 15 to 20 feet from the fence. Initially throw fly balls to provide more control to the drill.
- Fly balls can be thrown directly overhead, to the left or to the right of the outfielders.
- Remind outfielders about communicating with each other.

## PLAYER

- Pair up with another outfielder to take repetitions, aligning 20 to 30 yards apart and 15 to 20 feet from the fence.
- When the ball is hit or thrown, use the proper technique to get to the ball. Get to the fence quickly and then find the ball. Listen for your partner's communication regarding the fence.
- Once the catch is made, gather your feet to make a throw to the cut-off man.

# 65. Playing the Fence—Caroms/Bounces

**Primary Skill:** Fielding caroms and bounces

**Objective:** To practice fielding balls that carom or bounce off the outfield fence.

**Equipment Needed:** Six baseballs, gloves, a fungo bat and a fence

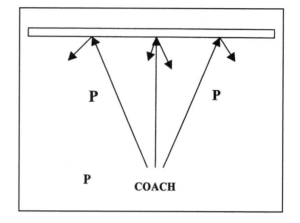

## COACH

- Talk through the technique and communication prior to the drill.

- Start with two outfielders taking repetitions 20 to 30 yards apart and 15 to 20 feet from the fence. Initially throw the balls to provide more control to the drill.

- Hit line drives or ground balls.

- Remind outfielders about communicating with each other.

## PLAYER

- Pair up with another outfielder to take repetitions, aligning 20 to 30 yards apart and 15 to 20 feet from the fence.

- When the ball gets by, play the ball off the fence, giving about 8 to 10 feet for a rebound or carom.

- Once the ball is caught, gather your feet to make a throw to the cut-off man.

# 66. Playing the Fence—Combo

**Primary Skill:** Fielding caroms, bounces and catching fly balls

**Objective:** To practice catching fly balls as well as playing caroms and bounces off the fence while developing communication between outfielders.

**Equipment Needed:** Six baseballs, gloves, a fungo bat and a fence

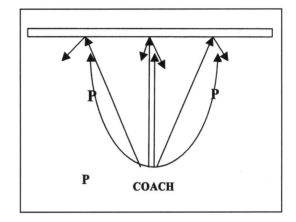

## COACH

- Talk through technique and communication prior to the drill.
- Start with two outfielders taking repetitions 20 to 30 yards apart and 15 to 20 feet from the fence. Initially throw the balls to provide more control to the drill.
- Hit line drives, ground balls or fly balls.
- Remind outfielders about communicating with each other.

## PLAYER

- Pair up with another outfielder to take repetitions, aligning 20 to 30 yards apart and 15 to 20 feet from the fence.
- When the ball gets by, play the ball off the fence giving about 8 to 10 feet for a rebound or carom. On fly balls, get to the fence quickly and then find the ball. Listen for your partner's communication regarding the fence.
- Once the ball is caught, gather your feet to make a throw to the cut-off man.

# 67. Sensational Catches

**Primary Skill:** Fielding and catching balls

**Objective:** To develop skill in turning and running for balls to the left, right or over your head.

**Equipment Needed:** Six baseballs, gloves, a fungo bat and a fence

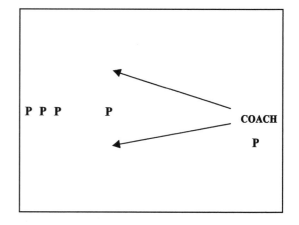

## COACH

- Talk through the drill before starting.

- Place the outfielders in a line, with one player stepping out in front to take repetitions. Another player stands 30 yards away to throw fly balls to left, right or behind the outfielder.

- Monitor the drill making sure the proper technique is being used.

## PLAYER

- Align in a single line, stepping out in front to take repetitions. Another player sets up 30 yards away to throw fly balls.

- Once the ball is caught, the thrower goes to the back of the line, while the catcher becomes the thrower.

# 68. Outfielders' Initial Steps

**Primary Skill:** Initial footwork

**Objective:** To develop the proper footwork on your initial reaction when tracking a ball to either side or directly behind you.

**Equipment Needed:** None

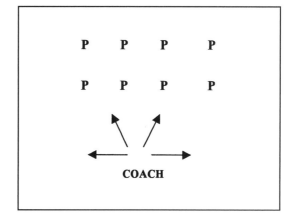

## COACH

- Align players in two or three rows with four across facing front. Allow plenty of space between each row and column.

- Stand approximately 20 feet in front of the group. Give the outfielders directions by hand movement—right, left or deep.

- Work through the drill for about 10 to 15 repetitions.

## PLAYER

- Align in rows of three or four across and two or three deep.

- Start in a good ready position, watching for the coach's hand signals. For hand movements to the left, use a crossover step to the left with the right foot, then reset. For hand movements to the right, use a crossover step with the left foot, then reset. For hand movements deep, pivot on either foot to face directly behind while crossing over with the other foot, then reset.

- On each hand movement take an initial step, then reset.

# 69. Outfielders' Footwork

**Primary Skill:** Footwork

**Objective:** To develop the proper footwork on your initial reaction when chasing a ball to either side or directly behind you.

**Equipment Needed:** Six baseballs and gloves

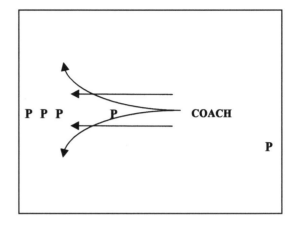

## COACH

- Create a single line with one player in front to take repetitions.

- Stand 16 to 20 yards from the players, giving a ready signal. Throw the ball either to the left, right or directly over the head of the player. Throwing the ball helps control the drill and allows monitoring of initial steps.

- Balls hit to either side should be attacked with a crossover step directly to the ball. For balls hit overhead, still use a crossover step, but pivot on the near foot directly to the ball, allowing hips to open for the crossover.

## PLAYER

- Stand in a single line, stepping out to take repetitions. Wait for the coach's ready signal to get into a good ready position.

- Once the ball is thrown, attack the ball by taking an initial crossover step toward the ball. For balls directly overhead, pivot on near foot, then crossover to the ball.

- Field the ball, gather your feet and throw the ball back to the coach.

**NOTE:** A good drill for indoor practices.

# 70. Tag-Ups

**Primary Skill:** Catching and throwing

**Objective:** To develop and reinforce the need to move forward through a fly ball while making a catch to gain the momentum needed to make a powerful throw.

**Equipment Needed:** Six baseballs, a fungo bat and gloves

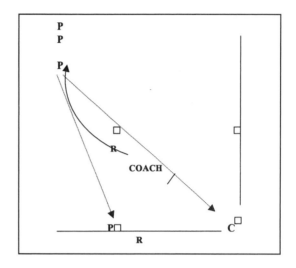

## COACH

- Place the outfielders in a single line in left, center or right field with one player out in front to take the repetition. Set up another player on second or third base, tagging up to move to next base. Incorporate infielders or catchers as well as extra outfielders to cover the throw coming to the bag or plate. If you use outfielders, make sure they rotate through the drill from outfielder to the runner to the player covering the base.

- Stand between the pitcher's mound and second base to hit fly balls. If it is too difficult to get the right fly balls off the bat, then move closer and throw fly balls. The important thing to remember is to give outfielders good fly balls to make this drill work.

- Monitor the techniques of the outfielders during the drill, making corrections and providing encouragement as well.

## PLAYER

- Set up in a single line in one of the outfield positions, stepping to the front to take repetitions. Another player needs to be positioned at a base to take throws from the outfielder performing the drill. Rotate through the drill after each repetition, going from outfielder to base coverage to the back of the line.

- At the beginning of each repetition, get into a good ready position, waiting for the coach to hit or throw a fly ball. Attack the ball, always keeping it slightly in front of you to provide movement through the ball while making the catch.

75

# 71. One-Hop Drill

**Primary Skill:** Long throwing

**Objective:** To develop throwing long and low, one-hopping the ball to the bag.

**Equipment Needed:** One baseball per pair and gloves

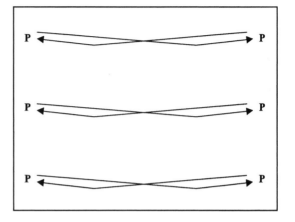

## COACH

- Demonstrate the technique and talk through the purpose prior to the drill.
- Pair up outfielders, each pair with one baseball, initially standing 20 yards apart.
- Monitor the throwing, having the players continue to create distance.
- Help the players determine the proper distance for long throwing and extending arms.

## PLAYER

- Pair up with another outfielder, starting 20 yards apart to loosen up.
- Continue to throw, moving apart as your arm warms up.
- Once at a distance where completing a throw on a fly is difficult, start throwing low line drives, one-hopping the ball to your partner.
- The goal is to throw the ball overhand with the proper spin so the ball has a long bounce to your partner.
- Your partner then returns a throw in the same manner. Repeat the drill 10 times.

# 72. Quick Start Drill

**Primary Skill:** Initial movement

**Objective:** To develop quick starts and movement toward the ball in any direction.

**Equipment Needed:** One baseball per pair

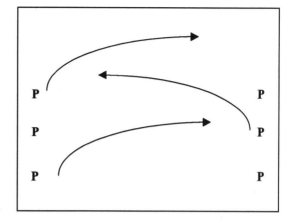

## COACH

- Demonstrate the purpose of the drill prior to the start.
- Pair players, aligning at 25 to 35 feet apart with one player throwing to the other.
- Circulate to all the pairs to encourage the proper technique.

## PLAYER

- Pair up with another outfielder with a baseball.
- Align about 25 to 35 feet apart, throwing balls over the left and right shoulder of your partner.
- When the ball is thrown over either shoulder, make a quick move to get to the ball. Catch the ball; gather your feet to make a throw.
- Return a throw to your partner in the same manner.

# 73. Relay Off the Fence

**Primary Skill:** Throwing to relay

**Objective:** To practice throwing to the relay man or cut-off after fielding a ball that bounced off the fence.

**Equipment Needed:** Six baseballs, gloves and a fence

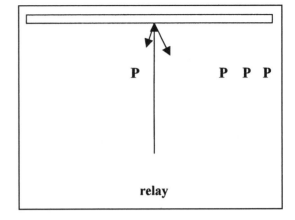

## COACH

- Place outfielders in a single line; the first player takes repetitions.
- Throw the ball off the fence, creating a rebound situation.
- Also place a relay man approximately 40 to 50 yards from fence.
- Make sure the outfielder's arms are warmed up prior to the drill.

## PLAYER

- Set up in a single line, with the first in line to take initial repetitions. Face the coach or thrower waiting for beginning of the repetition.
- When the ball is thrown off the fence, turn and field the ball. Then make a good throw to the relay man, right at head level, without a bounce.
- After the repetition, rotate to the relay man, while the relay man goes to the back of the line.

# 74. Ground Ball Drill (No One on Base)

**Primary Skill:** Fielding ground balls

**Objective:** To reinforce skills needed when fielding a ground ball in the outfield.

**Equipment Needed:** Six baseballs, gloves and a fungo bat

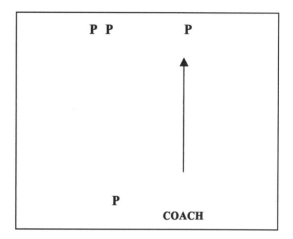

## COACH

- Demonstrate the proper technique prior to the drill.
- Put players in a single line, having the first player taking the initial repetitions.
- Stand approximately 30 yards from the outfielders. Throw a ground ball to the player taking repetitions.
- Work through the line four or five times.

## PLAYER

- Set up in a single line, stepping out in front to take repetitions.
- Start in a good ready position waiting for the coach to throw a ground ball.
- Field the ground ball, dropping down to one knee hooking the ball into your glove, then come up to make a throw back to the coach or player hitting the ball.

# 75. Ground Balls to Outfielders Positioned in the Infield

**Primary Skill:** Fielding ground balls

**Objective:** To develop and practice the skill of fielding ground balls.

**Equipment Needed:** Bag of baseballs, gloves, a fungo bat

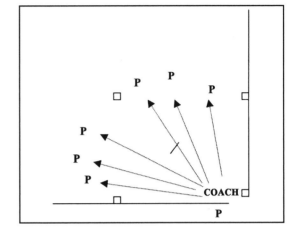

## COACH

- Demonstrate and coach the proper technique prior to and during the drill.

- Align outfielders in the infield, spreading them out.

- Hit ground balls to outfielders positioned in the infield. Have one player positioned next to the hitter to receive the throws from the outfielders.

## PLAYER

- Set up, covering the complete infield.

- When the coach or another player hits ground balls, use the proper technique to field the ball. Once the ball is fielded, make a good throw to the player next to the hitter.

**NOTE:** Use one section of the infield when space is limited. Place the outfielders in a single line.

# 76. Right-of-Way Drill

**Primary Skill:** Communication

**Objective:** To practice and develop communication between the outfielders.

**Equipment Needed:** Six baseballs, a fungo bat and gloves

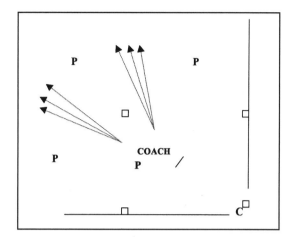

## COACH

- Talk through the purpose of the drill prior to the start.

- Set up the outfielders in positions: left, center and right.

- Throw or hit fly balls between the outfielders, causing them to communicate. Once the ball is fielded, have the outfielder make a return throw.

## PLAYER

- Align in regular outfield positions waiting for the coach to throw or hit a fly ball in the gap.

- Once the ball is in the air, attack the fly ball and communicate with the other outfielder. The center fielder has the right-of-way on any ball that the center fielder can catch.

- Catch the ball, and then make a return throw to the player next to the coach.

# 77. Classroom—Initial Step

**Primary Skill:** Initial movement

**Objective:** To practice and reinforce the initial steps when moving toward the ball in the outfield.

**Equipment Needed:** None

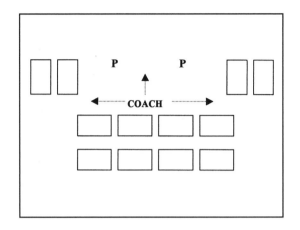

## COACH

- Clear a spot by moving a few desks to the side. Set two players at a time due to limited space.

- Give the players directions to take an initial step left, right or deep.

- Work through outfielders three or four times.

## PLAYER

- Step up into the cleared area to take repetitions. Get in a good ready position, waiting for the coach's signal.

- When the coach gives a signal, take an initial step in the same direction, taking a crossover step with your opposite foot. Reset and wait for the next repetition.

# 78. Classroom—Fly Ball Body Position

**Primary Skill:** Fly ball body position

**Objective:** To practice the proper body position when fielding fly balls.

**Equipment Needed**: Gloves

## COACH

- Demonstrate the proper technique prior to the start of the drill.
- Clear an area by moving desks to the side of the room. Set two players at a time due to limited space.
- Give the players a signal to take an initial step to get into the proper position to catch a fly ball.
- Work through outfielders three or four times.

## PLAYER

- Step up into the cleared area to take repetitions. Get in a good ready position and wait for the coach's signal.
- When the coach gives a signal, take an initial step to get into the proper body position to field a fly ball. Reset and wait for the next repetition.

# 79. Throws to the Bag

**Primary Skill:** Throws to cut-off man and/or base

**Objective:** To practice and reinforce throws to the cut-off man and/or base.

**Equipment Needed:** Six baseballs, a fungo bat, gloves and bases

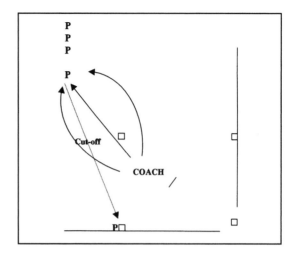

## COACH

- Talk through the drill prior to the start.
- Place outfielders in one of the outfield positions in a single line. One outfielder can start as the cut-off man; another starts at the base to which throws will be made.
- Instruct the outfielders to throw the ball toward the cut-off man with enough velocity to make it to the bag. The man covering the bag needs to communicate whether the ball should be cut off or let through.
- Hit fly balls or ground balls to the outfielders during each repetition.
- Rotate the players through the drill from the outfield to the cut-off, to covering the bag, to end of the line.

## PLAYER

- Set up in a single line in one of the outfield positions. Step out in front to take repetitions, while another player takes the cut-off position and another covers the bag to which throws will be made.
- Start in a good ready position waiting for the coach to hit the ball, either a fly ball or ground ball.
- Once the ball is fielded, come up throwing toward the cut-off man's head. Release the throw with enough velocity to make it to the bag if it is not cut off.
- Take a repetition in the outfield, then rotate to cut-off man and then cover the bag.
- When covering the bag, communicate to the cut-off man whether to cut off the ball or let it go through.

# 80. Fly Balls to the Left

**Primary Skill:** Catching fly balls on the run

**Objective:** To practice catching fly balls to your left while on the run.

**Equipment Needed:** Six baseballs, gloves, a fungo bat

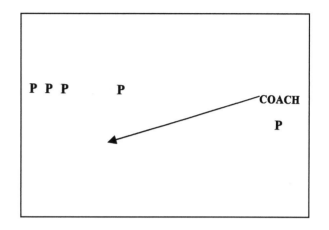

## COACH

- Set up the players in a single line in the outfield with one player stepping forward to take repetitions.
- Stand approximately 50 yards from the outfielders, hitting fly balls to the left of the players.
- Give each outfielder three to five repetitions through the drill.

## PLAYER

- Align in a single line in the outfield, stepping forward to take the repetitions.
- Get into a good ready position prior to the ball being hit. Once the ball is in the air, take a crossover step in the direction of the ball.
- Try to get under the ball if possible and use good form when making the catch.
- If this is not possible, run the ball down, making the catch on the run. As soon as the catch is made, gather your feet to make a good throw to the cut-off or player receiving throws from the outfielders.

# 81. Fly Balls to the Right

**Primary Skill:** Catching fly balls on the run

**Objective:** To practice catching fly balls to your right while on the run.

**Equipment Needed:** Six baseballs, gloves, a fungo bat

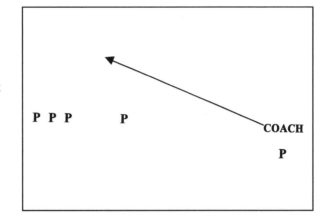

## COACH

- Set up the players in a single line in the outfield with one player stepping forward to take the repetitions.
- Stand approximately 50 yards from the outfielders, hitting fly balls to the right of the players.
- Give each outfielder three to five repetitions through the drill.

## PLAYER

- Align in a single line in the outfield, stepping forward to take repetitions.
- Get into a good ready position prior to the ball being hit. Once the ball is in the air, take a crossover step in the direction of the ball.
- Attempt to get under the ball if possible and use good form when making the catch.
- If this is not possible, run the ball down, making the catch on the run. As soon as the catch is made, gather your feet to make a good throw to the cut-off or player receiving throws from the outfielders.

# 82. Ground Balls to the Left

**Primary Skill:** Fielding ground balls on the run

**Objective:** To practice fielding ground balls to your left while on the run.

**Equipment Needed:** Six baseballs, gloves, a fungo bat

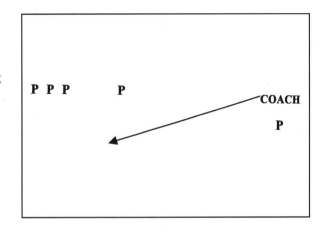

## COACH

- Set up the players in a single line in the outfield with one player stepping forward to take the repetitions.
- Stand approximately 50 yards from the outfielders, hitting ground balls to the left of the players.
- Give each outfielder three to five repetitions through the drill.

## PLAYER

- Align in a single line in the outfield, stepping forward to take repetitions.
- Get into a good ready position prior to the ball being hit. Once the ball is hit, take a crossover step in the direction of the ball.
- Try to get in front of the ball if possible and use good form when fielding.
- If this is not possible, run the ball down, fielding it on the run. As soon as the ball is gloved, gather your feet to make a good throw to the cut-off or player receiving throws from the outfielders.

# 83. Ground Balls to the Right

**Primary Skill:** Fielding ground balls on the run

**Objective:** To practice fielding ground balls to the right while on the run.

**Equipment Needed:** Six baseballs, gloves, a fungo bat

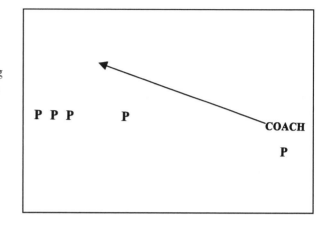

## COACH

- Set up players in a single line in the outfield with one player stepping forward to take the repetitions.

- Stand approximately 50 yards from outfielders, hitting ground balls to the right of the players.

- Give each outfielder three to five repetitions through the drill.

## PLAYER

- Align in a single line in the outfield, stepping forward to take repetitions.

- Get into a good ready position prior to the ball being hit. Once the ball is hit, take a crossover step in the direction of the ball.

- Try to get in front of the ball if possible and use good form when fielding.

- If this is not possible, run the ball down, fielding it on the run. As soon as ball is gloved, gather your feet to make a good throw to the cut-off or player receiving throws from the outfielders.

# SECTION 3

# PITCHING

*You must never, never, never quit.*

—WINSTON CHURCHILL

# 84. Long Toss

**Primary Skill:** Loosening, strengthening and stretching the arm

**Objective:** To loosen, strengthen and stretch the throwing arm.

**Equipment Needed:** One baseball per pair and gloves

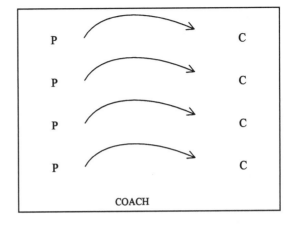

## COACH

- Set up either in left field or right field, throwing from the foul line to center field. Pair up the pitchers with each other or with a catcher.

- Perform the drill during warm-ups prior to pitching workouts or during pregame with the catcher. This is a good drill for the catchers as well.

## PLAYER

- Pair up with another pitcher or a catcher, setting up in left field or right field, throwing from the foul line to center field.

- After loosening and preliminary warm-ups, extend the throwing distance gradually to approximately 50 yards.

- Throw the ball with an arc to your partner; the idea is to stretch and loosen the throwing arm, not to add stress.

# 85. Five-Step Drill

**Primary Skill:** Windup pitching motion

**Objective:** To practice and reinforce the proper technique throughout each phase of the pitching motion.

**Equipment Needed:** Athletic tape, baseball gloves

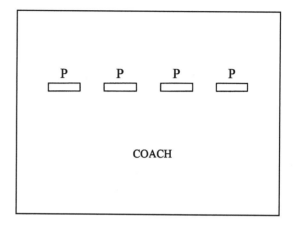

## COACH

- Set up on the diamond or in the gym with the pitchers. Use tape on the gym floor to simulate a pitching rubber. Outside, use a mark on the ground or other objects to simulate the pitching rubber.
- Pitchers should be facing the coach in a ready position without baseballs.
- A cue is given to the pitchers to move through each phase of the windup.
- Start slowly. Have the pitchers hold each step for a few seconds in order to check the technique. Pick up the pace as the pitchers feel more confident with the motion.

## PLAYER

- Align on makeshift pitching rubbers facing the coach.
- Wait for the coach's cue to start the windup and progress to each phase.
- The initial movement is a small, short drop step behind the rubber.
- Next is a square-off step or block step with a plant.
- Move to the balance position or power position. Raise the knee to the chest with the foot relaxed.
- Stride toward home plate while extending the throwing arm toward second base.
- Finally, complete the throwing motion and the follow-through.

# 86. One-Knee Follow-Through

**Primary Skill:** Follow-through

**Objective:** To practice and reinforce the proper follow-through after the release of the ball.

**Equipment Needed:** One baseball per pair and gloves

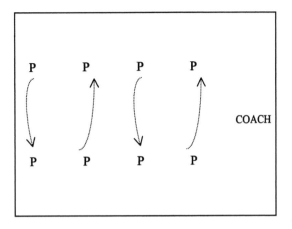

## COACH

- Set up on the diamond or in the gym with the pitchers paired with each other.

- Demonstrate the proper follow-through to the players prior to the drill.

- Emphasize the follow-through and not the throw, making sure the pitchers are not firing the ball at each other.

- Monitor each pair for good form.

## PLAYER

- Face partner kneeling on the plant foot leg. Place the other leg in front of your body at a 45-degree angle approximately with the foot on the ground, the knee in front of the chest.

- Focus on reaching toward second base with the ball, with good arm extension and the elbow at shoulder height, and throw downhill.

- Follow-through by bringing the arm across to the opposite knee. The arm will end up in front of the opposite shin.

- Throws do not need to be hard for this drill; the speed of the throw is not important.

# 87. Balance While Throwing

**Primary Skill:** Balance position in pitching motion

**Objective:** To practice and reinforce the balance/power position during the pitching motion.

**Equipment Needed:** One baseball per pitcher or pair

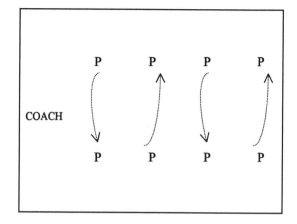

## COACH

- Demonstrate the proper technique prior to the start of the drill.

- Monitor the drill, making sure the pitchers are tucking their lead knee to their chest with the foot relaxed.

- Emphasize that the knee must stay parallel to the rubber and not go behind.

## PLAYER

- Start in the balance position:

    —The front shoulder facing home plate.
    —The plant foot squared off in front of rubber.
    —The front knee tucked.
    —The front foot relaxed.

- Focus on balance, the leg tuck, reaching for home plate with the front foot, the elbow shoulder height, with good arm extension to second base and a good follow-through.

- Ball speed is not important when throwing to partner.

**NOTE:** Incorporate this drill with the pitcher workouts. Also when the pitchers are warming up with each other, they can start from this position.

# 88. Towel Drill

**Primary Skill:** Wrist snap and follow-through in pitching motion

**Objective:** To reinforce the wrist snap and follow-through during the pitching motion.

**Equipment Needed:** Three or four quarter pieces of towels or rags and three or four pitching rubbers

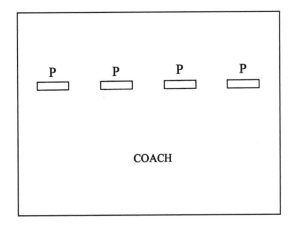

## COACH

- Talk through the purpose of the drill and demonstrate the proper technique.
- Use rags, quarter pieces of old towels or even old socks.
- Have the pitchers go through a complete motion using the towels as the ball.
- Use in conjunction with other pitching drills.

## PLAYER

- Face the coach with the towels between the first two fingers of the throwing hand.
- Proceed through the pitching motion—perform the complete motion using the towels in place of a ball.
- Snap the towel with the wrist during the follow-through of the motion.

**NOTE:** The snapping of the towel helps develop good wrist action during the pitching motion.

# 89. Target Drill

**Primary Skill:** Accuracy for pitchers

**Objective:** To develop accuracy when pitching and spotting the ball in the strike zone.

**Equipment Needed:** Baseballs, netting or screen, home plates and tape or shoestrings

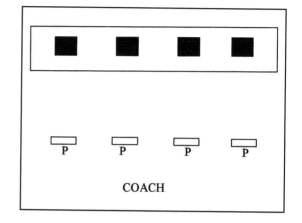

## COACH

- Use the sides of the batting cage or individual pitching screens.

- Tape or weave colored shoestrings to form a target on the screen approximately the height and width of the strike zone. Commercial screens already designed for this purpose can be purchased.

- Use for pitchers struggling to hit the strike zone; also use with all pitchers during preseason workouts.

- Monitor the number of pitches the pitchers throw during this drill.

## PLAYER

- Align in front of a target the approximate distance of the pitching rubber from the target.

- Focus on the proper technique during the pitching motion and on hitting the strike zone.

- After working on hitting the strike zone, work on spotting the ball in different locations of the strike zone.

**NOTE:** To make the drill competitive, assign points for each strike thrown by the pitchers competing in the drill.

# 90. Bag Drill

**Primary Skill:** Accuracy for pitchers

**Objective:** To develop accuracy and comfort throwing with a batter standing in the batter's box.

**Equipment Needed:** One baseball per pitcher, gloves, catcher's gear, home plates, pitching rubbers and a blocking bag or rubber trash can

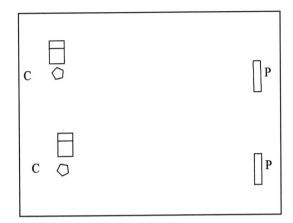

## COACH

- Set up the drill in the gym or on the field with a pitcher and a catcher.
- Stand a blocking bag in one of the batter's boxes, switching after a designated number of pitches.
- If the bags are not available, use rubber trash cans or a pitching screen.
- Monitor pitcher's technique throughout the drill as well as the number of pitches thrown. Also provide encouragement whenever possible.

## PLAYER

- Pair up with a catcher. Work on pitching mechanics as well as location.
- The coach will indicate the number of pitches that should be thrown during the drill.
- Focus on technique and throwing to a target not on the batter.

**NOTE:** The simulated batter helps to develop confidence without the anxiety of possibly hitting batters.

# 91. Preseason Throwing

**Primary Skill:** Development of throwing arm

**Objective:** To strengthen and develop the pitcher's arm leading up to the season.

**Equipment Needed:** One baseball per pitcher, gloves, catcher's gear, home plates and pitching rubbers

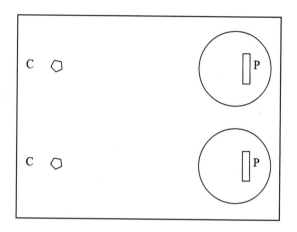

## COACH

- Pair the pitchers with the catchers, creating a schedule prior to practice—rotate the catchers.
- Commit the pitchers to this schedule, even if they are also position players.
- Monitor the pitchers as much as possible. Create expectations for the pitchers during this time period.

## PLAYER

- First, check the coach's schedule for time slot and the catcher. Also, check expectations for pitching workout.
- Concentrate on good pitching mechanics, as well as working on different pitches, but stay with a majority of fastballs.

**NOTE:** Refer to preseason pitching schedule below.

### PRESEASON PITCHING SCHEDULE

Week #1:  Days One through Three
26 pitches (1/2 to 3/4 speed)
1/2 windup, 1/2 stretch
All fastballs, work on motion

Days Four and Five
36 pitches (1/2 to 3/4 speed, full speed last 10)
1/2 windup, 1/2 stretch
All fastballs, work on motion

Rest two days

Week #3:  Throw in two scrimmages
(three innings or 50 pitches)
Intersquad or other
Few days apart

Week #2:  Days One and Two
36 pitches (normal speed)
1/2 windup, 1/2 stretch
3/4 fastballs, 1/4 other pitches

Days Three through Five
Throw batting practice (be aware of the number of pitches and batters)

Rest two days

Week #4:  Start of the season
In-season workout should consist of 25 to 30 pitches (following above pattern)

# 92. Pick-Off Options

**Primary Skill:** Pick-off moves

**Objective:** To practice options when holding a runner close to first base.

**Equipment Needed:** One baseball per pitcher, gloves and a base

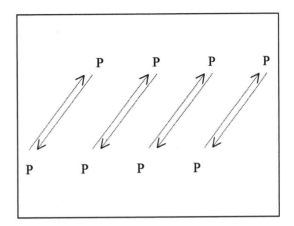

## COACH

- Set up on the field or in the gym with the pitchers paired with each other.
- Have partners at a 45-degree angle from each other, approximately the distance from the pitcher's mound to first base.
- Talk through and demonstrate the options prior to the start of the drill.
- Monitor pairs, each should be practicing all the options.

## PLAYER

- Pair up and align at a 45-degree angle in relationship to a partner.
- While one works from the stretch, the other simulates being a first baseman.
- Perform moves full speed after a few repetitions of the walk-throughs. Keep the arm positioning and feet movement in mind during repetitions.

# 93. Fielding Bunts

**Primary Skill:** Fielding bunts

**Objective:** To practice and reinforce the proper fielding and throwing techniques for pitchers coming off the mound to field bunts.

**Equipment Needed:** Six baseballs, gloves and a base

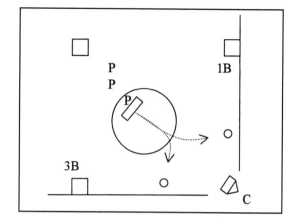

## COACH

- Talk through and demonstrate the technique prior to the start of the drill.
- Set up on the diamond or in the gym with the pitchers on a mound.
- Use the pitcher's mound to combine the proper fielding of a bunt and throwing to a base. The ball can be spotted or rolled to simulate a live bunt.

## PLAYER

- Pitchers start from either a windup or stretch position, simulating a pitch by going through the motion.
- Move to field the bunted ball after performing the pitching motion, continue to throw to base if directed by coach.

**NOTE:** The ball should be fielded with both hands together, keeping the ball slightly in front between the feet. If the ball has stopped, the pitcher can field it with a bare hand by pushing straight down on the ball as the grasp is being made.

# 94. Spin Drill

**Primary Skill:** Ball spin

**Objective:** To practice and reinforce placing the proper spin on the ball for different types of pitches.

**Equipment Needed:** A baseball, gloves and a home plate

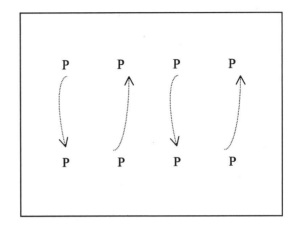

## COACH

• Demonstrate the technique and explain the purpose of the drill prior to the start.
• Pair the pitchers, each pair having one baseball and aligning approximately 30 feet apart.
• One pitcher will perform the drill while the other gets down on one knee as if he were the catcher and checks for the proper spin on the pitch being thrown.
• Pitchers should throw 10 to 15 repetitions before switching. Monitor the pitchers, checking for the proper mechanics as well as providing encouragement.

## PLAYER

• Pair up with another pitcher or catcher, aligning approximately 30 feet apart with one baseball for the pair. One should be throwing, working on different pitches, while the other is on one knee catching.
• Start with the front leg planted as if the stride has already been completed; the lead toe should be opened to the target while the front shoulder and hips stay closed.
• The front arm should be slightly bent, shoulder height, while the throwing arm should swing to the throwing position shoulder height.
• From this position, throw the pitch to the catcher with a good follow-through motion, lifting the back leg and dropping it parallel to the front foot.
• Communicate with the catcher regarding the type of pitch that is being thrown so the spin can be monitored. Also, the ball should only be thrown half to three-quarter speed because of the distance and the focus of the drill.
• If paired up with another pitcher, take 10 to 15 repetitions before switching.

**NOTE:** This is a good drill for pregame warm-ups for the pitchers. It helps to loosen up the pitchers, as well as reinforce the proper mechanics.

# 95. Backing Up Bases

**Primary Skill:** Back up

**Objective:** To practice backing up throws to second base, third base and home plate.

**Equipment Needed:** Six baseballs, gloves and bases

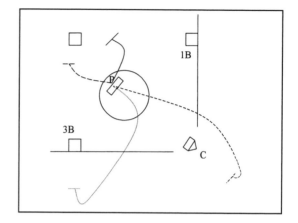

## COACH

- Demonstrate and talk through the purpose of the drill prior to the start.

- Place a pitcher on the pitcher's mound with extra pitchers covering second base, third base and home plate.

- Stand in one of the outfield positions about 30 feet deep. Give the pitchers a situation prior to throwing the ball.

- Start the drill by having the pitcher perform the windup or stretch motion; once this is completed, throw the ball to the appropriate base. Make a bad throw from time to time to cause the ball to get by the player covering the bag.

- Remind pitchers to think two bases ahead prior to the throw.

- Have the pitchers take three repetitions before rotating to a bag-coverage position.

## PLAYER

- Start on the mound, while other pitchers cover second base, third base and home plate. Listen for the coach's situations prior to starting the pitching motion.

- Start the drill by performing the pitching motion either from the stretch or the windup without a ball. Once the motion is completed, move to the proper back-up position on the field. This will depend on the situation presented by the coach.

- Take three repetitions before rotating to one of the bag-coverage positions.

# 96. Follow-Through Drill

**Primary Skill:** Follow-through

**Objective:** To practice and reinforce follow-through during the pitching motion.

**Equipment Needed:** A baseball and gloves

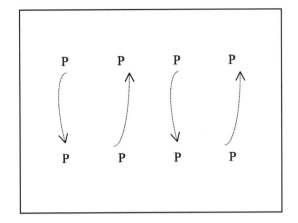

## COACH

- Demonstrate the technique and explain the purpose of the drill prior to the start.
- Pair the pitchers, each pair having one baseball and aligning approximately 30 feet apart. The pitchers can also pair up with catcher.
- One pitcher will perform the drill with a partner, then the partner will perform the same technique.
- Pitchers should throw 10 to 15 repetitions. Monitor pitchers, checking for proper mechanics as well as providing encouragement.

## PLAYER

- Pair up with another pitcher or a catcher, aligning approximately 30 feet apart with one baseball.
- Start with the front leg planted as if you already completed the stride; the lead toe should be opened to the target while the front shoulder and hips stay closed.
- The front arm should be slightly bent at shoulder height, while the throwing arm should swing to the throwing position at shoulder height.
- From this position, throw the pitch to the catcher with a good follow-through motion, lifting the back leg and dropping it parallel to the front foot.
- The ball should only be thrown half to three-quarter speed because of the distance and the focus of the drill.
- If paired up with another pitcher, take 10 to 15 repetitions before switching.

**NOTE:** This is a good drill for pregame warm-ups for the pitchers. It helps to loosen up the pitchers as well as reinforce the proper mechanics.

# 97. Covering First Base

**Primary Skill:** First base coverage

**Objective:** To practice first base coverage by the pitcher on a ball hit to the right side of the infield.

**Equipment Needed:** Six baseballs, a base and gloves

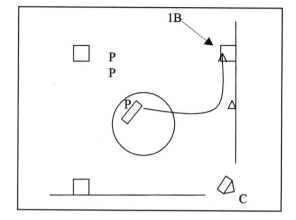

## COACH

- Demonstrate the proper technique prior to the start of the drill.
- Congregate the pitchers at the pitcher's mound, one starting on the pitching rubber performing the windup or the stretch motion.
- Stand in a normal first baseman's position or somewhere in that proximity with six baseballs. Give the pitcher a starting signal to begin the pitch; after the pitching motion is performed, the pitcher then takes the proper angle to cover first base for a throw.
- As the pitcher approaches the bag, make a toss either underhand or overhand.
- During the drill, monitor the pitcher's technique and path to first base for the throw.

## PLAYER

- Align at the pitcher's mound, with one player taking initial repetitions starting on the pitching rubber.
- Perform either a windup or the stretch motion; once the motion is completed break to first base to cover the bag on a ball hit to the right side of the infield.
- Use the proper approach to the first base bag while looking for a throw from the coach.
- After the repetition move to the back of the line.

# 98. Covering Bases on Fly Balls

**Primary Skill:** Covering bases

**Objective:** To reinforce base coverage by the pitcher on a fly ball to the infield.

**Equipment Needed:** Six baseballs, bases and gloves

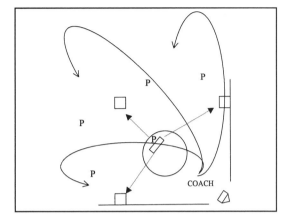

## COACH

• Talk through the purpose of the drill and situation when base coverage is needed.

• Place one pitcher on the mound ready to start the pitching motion either from the windup or the stretch. Place the other pitchers at infield positions to catch the fly balls.

• Stand behind the pitcher's mound with six baseballs to throw fly balls to different positions in the infield. After the pitcher goes through the windup or the stretch, throw a fly ball to a deep infield position.

• Monitor the pitcher's movement to the appropriate base for coverage after throwing a fly ball.

## PLAYER

• Assemble at the pitcher's mound on the rubber ready to perform the windup or the stretch. Extra pitchers align in regular infield positions fielding fly balls from the coach.

• Start the drill by going through the windup or the stretch motion, then look for a fly ball thrown by the coach to a deep infield position. Cover the appropriate base depending upon the position of the fly ball.

• Take a repetition and then rotate through the fielding positions.

# 99. Comeback Ball—Throwing to First

**Primary Skill:** Throwing the ball to first base

**Objective:** To practice throwing the ball to first base on a comeback ball hit to the pitcher.

**Equipment Needed:** Six baseballs, gloves, a fungo bat and a base

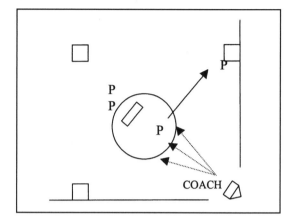

## COACH

- Talk through the drill and demonstrate the proper mechanics when making a throw to first base.

- Place pitchers at the pitcher's mound with one player standing on the rubber ready to go through the windup or the stretch motion. Another pitcher plays first base waiting for throws from the mound.

- Stand at home plate with six baseballs and a fungo bat to hit ground balls to the pitcher. After the pitcher fields the ball, a throw then should be made to first base using the proper mechanics.

- Rotate the pitchers after each repetition, with players moving to first base after pitching.

- Monitor the pitchers; provide encouragement during the drill.

## PLAYER

- Start at the pitcher's mound while another pitcher covers the first base bag for throws.

- Begin the drill by going through the windup or the stretch motion. After following through, field the ground ball hit by the coach. Once the ball is fielded, turn to first base to make a good throw to the bag. Use the proper mechanics.

- After taking a repetition on the mound, rotate to first base and then to the back of the line.

# 100. Comeback Ball—Throwing to Second Base

**Primary Skill:** Throwing the ball to second base

**Objective:** To practice throwing the ball to second base on a comeback hit to the pitcher.

**Equipment Needed:** Six baseballs, gloves, a fungo bat and a base

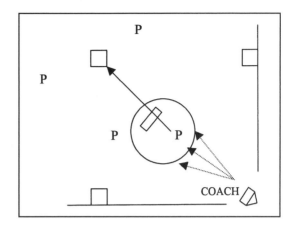

## COACH

- Talk through the drill and demonstrate the proper mechanics when making a throw to second base.
- Place the pitchers at the pitcher's mound with one player standing on the rubber ready to go through the windup or the stretch motion. Other pitchers play second base and shortstop waiting for throws from the mound.
- Stand at home plate with six baseballs and a fungo bat to hit ground balls to the pitcher. After the pitcher fields the ball, a throw then should be made to second base using the proper mechanics. Make sure the pitcher communicates with the second baseman or shortstop before starting each repetition.
- Rotate the pitchers after each repetition, moving to second base after pitching.
- Monitor the pitchers; provide encouragement during the drill.

## PLAYER

- Start at the pitcher's mound while the other pitchers play second and shortstop for throws to the second base bag.
- Begin the drill by communicating with the shortstop and second baseman, then go through the windup or the stretch motion. After following through, field the ground ball hit by the coach. Once the ball is fielded turn to second base and make a good throw to the bag. Use the proper mechanics.
- After taking a repetition on the mound, rotate to second base, then to shortstop and then to the back of the line.

# 101. Premature Break by Base Runner

**Primary Skill:** Defense

**Objective:** To practice and reinforce defending against a premature break by a base runner.

**Equipment Needed:** Six baseballs, gloves and bases

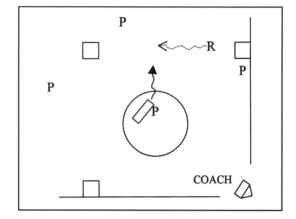

## COACH

- Talk through and demonstrate the proper technique prior to the start of the drill.
- Place the pitchers at the pitcher's mound with one player standing on the rubber ready to go through the stretch motion. Other pitchers can rotate as the base runners—either between first and second, second and third or third and home—as well as the infielders.
- As the pitcher starts the stretch motion, the runner should start walking or running off the base to create a premature break to the next base.
- When the situation is recognized, the pitcher steps off the rubber and runs at the base runner, making the runner commit in either direction.
- Alternate what the base runner does. One time the base runner should break early, the next time the base runner holds during the pitch.
- The pitchers can take three repetitions at a time; this will give you an opportunity to mix up the situations. Also, alternate the base runners at first, second and third.
- Monitor the drill closely, providing corrections and encouragement as needed.

## PLAYER

- Start at the pitcher's mound while the other pitchers step in as base runners and infielders.
- Begin the drill by starting on the rubber from the stretch position. Start the stretch motion keeping an eye on the runner. As soon as the runner breaks for the next base, step off the rubber and run directly at the runner, keeping the ball in your throwing hand.
- Take three repetitions before rotating to an infield position or being a base runner. The coach will mix up the situations during the repetitions.

# 102. Premature Break by Base Runner—First and Third

**Primary Skill:** Defense

**Objective:** To practice and reinforce defending against a premature break by a base runner during a first and third situation.

**Equipment Needed:** Six baseballs, gloves and bases

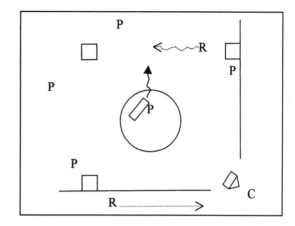

## COACH

• Talk through and demonstrate the proper technique prior to the start of the drill.

• Place the pitchers at the pitcher's mound with one player standing on the rubber ready to go through the stretch motion. Other pitchers can rotate as the base runners either at first base or third base as well as infielders and catcher.

• As the pitcher starts the stretch motion, the runner on first base should start walking or running off the base to create a premature break to second base.

• When the situation is recognized, the pitcher steps off the rubber and runs at the base runner, staying aware of the runner on third base. When the runner on third breaks for home, the pitcher turns and throws to the catcher.

• Alternate what the base runner does. One time the base runner breaks early, the next time the base runner holds during the pitch.

• The pitchers can take three repetitions at a time; this will give you an opportunity to mix up the situations.

• Monitor the drill closely, providing corrections and encouragement as needed.

## PLAYER

• Start at the pitcher's mound while the other pitchers step in as the base runners, infielders and catcher.

• Begin the drill by starting on the rubber from the stretch position. Start the stretch motion but keep an eye on the runner. As soon as the runner breaks for the next base, step off the rubber and run directly at the runner, keeping the ball in your throwing hand. Listen for communication about the runner breaking to home; as soon as this happens, turn and make an accurate throw to the catcher.

• Take three repetitions before rotating to an infield position or being a base runner. The coach will mix up the situations during the repetitions.

# 103. Bunt Reaction Drill

**Primary Skill:** Fielding bunts

**Objective:** To practice fielding bunts and throwing to different bases.

**Equipment Needed:** Six baseballs, four bases and gloves

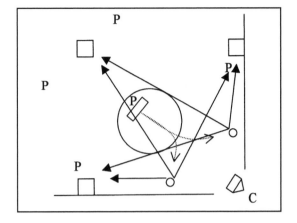

## COACH

- Set four bases in the gym to simulate an infield. Align the pitchers in the middle, facing one of the bases, which will become home plate. Extra pitchers will cover the infield bases and home plate.

- The pitcher taking repetitions goes from the stretch and throws home. The player catching the ball rolls the ball toward first or third simulating a bunt and then calls out a base.

- The pitcher fields the ball, then throws to the base identified. Have the pitchers take three repetitions before switching and rotating to cover the bases.

- Monitor the mechanics and provide encouragement throughout the drill.

## PLAYER

- Set up in the middle of the four bases facing the base that will become home plate. The other pitchers become infielders and cover each base and another becomes the catcher.

- Start from the stretch, throwing the ball to the catcher. When the catcher rolls the ball, field the ball and listen for the catcher to identify a base.

- After three repetitions, rotate to the infield and catcher positions.

# 104. Curve Ball Drill

**Primary Skill:** Throwing a curve ball

**Objective:** To practice putting the proper spin on the curve ball.

**Equipment Needed:** A baseball and gloves

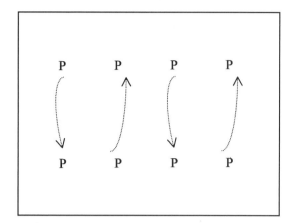

## COACH

- Draw a stripe between the seams in the same direction the seams are going or paint one panel between the seams.

- Pair the pitchers and set them up about 30 feet apart. Each pair should have a striped ball.

- One pitcher throws a curve ball to a partner, looking for the stripe to have an overspin. If stripe is spinning on the side, hand position was wrong.

- Monitor pairs, checking spin and making corrections when needed.

## PLAYER

- Pair up with another pitcher standing about 30 feet apart. Use a striped ball during the drill.

- Throw a curve ball to your partner, looking for the proper overspin of the striped ball. Your partner will then return a throw in the same manner. If the stripe is spinning on the side of the ball, the fingers are not staying on top of the ball.

- Take about 10 to 15 throws to your partner.

# 105. Double Bunt Drill

**Primary Skill:** Fielding bunts

**Objective:** To practice fielding bunts and throwing to first or third base.

**Equipment Needed:** One baseball per pair, gloves and two bases

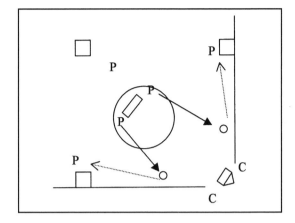

## COACH

- Talk through the drill prior to the start. Pair two pitchers, one in each set serving as the catcher. Use other pitchers to cover first and third base.
- Place two pitchers about 10 to 15 feet apart side by side with the catchers at normal distance and the same proximity as the pitchers. First and third base should be at the normal distance also.
- Both pitchers start from the stretch position throwing to the catcher. After receiving the ball, the catcher will then roll the ball out toward first or third base. The pitcher on the right side of the mound fields the ball and throws to third base, while the pitcher on the left side of the mound fields the ball and throws to first base.
- After each pitcher takes a repetition from one side, switch and perform a repetition from the other side before rotating to the other positions.
- Monitor the drill closely, making corrections and providing encouragement when needed.

## PLAYER

- Pair up with another pitcher who will be about 10 to 15 feet away. Other pitchers will be the catchers the same distance apart, while two other pitchers will cover first and third base for throws.
- Begin the drill from the stretch position throwing to the catcher. As soon as the catcher receives the ball, it will be rolled back. The catcher on the first base side will roll it toward first, while the catcher on the third base side will roll the ball toward third.
- Once the ball is rolled, field it and throw it to the closest base. The pitcher on the right fields the ball and throws to third base, while the pitcher on the left fields the ball and throws to first base.
- After taking a repetition from one side, switch and perform a repetition from the other side before rotating to the other positions.

# 106. Running Foul Poles

**Primary Skill:** Conditioning

**Objective:** To warm up as well as condition the pitchers before the game and during practice.

**Equipment Needed:** None

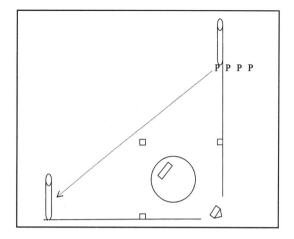

## COACH

- Place the pitchers at either the right field foul pole or the left field foul pole to start.

- Have them run half to three-quarter speed to the opposite foul pole. Once the destination is reached, have the pitchers rest for 20 to 30 seconds and repeat the repetition.

- The pitchers should initially run five poles; as the season progresses increase the repetitions to 10 or more. If this is being done as a warm-up for pregame, limit the amount of repetitions.

## PLAYER

- Line up at either the right field foul pole or the left field foul pole to start.

- Run half to three-quarter speed to the opposite foul pole. Once the destination is reached, rest for 20 to 30 seconds and repeat the repetition.

- Run five poles; as the season progresses increase the repetitions to 10 or more. During pregame warm-ups, limit the amount of repetitions.

# 107. Double Ball Drill

**Primary Skill:** Conditioning

**Objective:** To condition the pitchers during the preseason as well as in-season.

**Equipment Needed:** Two baseballs per pair

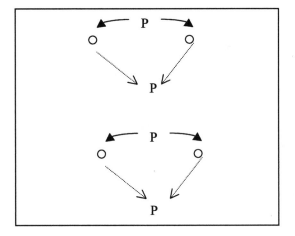

## COACH

- Demonstrate the technique prior to the start of the drill.
- Pair the pitchers with each pair having two baseballs and standing about 10 feet apart. One pitcher will be the roller, while the other performs the drill.
- The player rolling the balls will roll a ball to the other player's left or right. As the player fields the ball and flips it back to the roller, the other ball should be on its way.
- Repeat repetitions 10 to 15 times before switching.

## PLAYER

- Pair up with another pitcher standing about 10 feet apart with two baseballs.
- Get into a good balance stance with feet shoulder width apart, bending at the waist and hands out in front.
- When your partner rolls a ball to the left or right, move to the ball and field it. Flip it back to your partner, looking for the other ball to be rolled immediately.
- Continue drill for about 10 to 15 repetitions before switching.

# 108. Slide-Step Drill

**Primary Skill:** Stride

**Objective:** To practice and reinforce the slide step by the pitcher during the stretch motion.

**Equipment Needed:** One baseball per pair

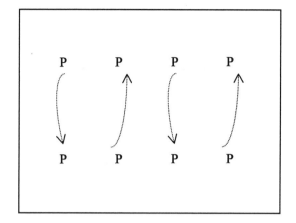

## COACH

- Demonstrate the proper technique prior to the drill.

- Pair pitchers standing about 30 feet apart with one baseball. Each pitcher, when throwing, will start from the stretch position.

- The first pitcher will start from the stretch position when taking the stride to throw; the front foot will slide toward a target just off the ground as a throw is being made.

- The other pitcher returns a throw in the same manner. Have the pitchers continue the drill for about 10 to 15 repetitions.

- Monitor drill closely, making corrections when needed.

## PLAYER

- Pair up with another pitcher standing about 30 feet apart.

- Start from the stretch position. When striding to your target, slide your front foot just off the ground as a throw is being made.

- The other pitcher returns a throw in the same manner. Take about 10 to 15 repetitions.

# 109. Spot Drill

© 2001 by Prentice Hall

**Primary Skill:** Location

**Objective:** To practice spotting the baseball in different locations in the strike zone.

**Equipment Needed:** Catcher's gear, glove, a baseball and home plate

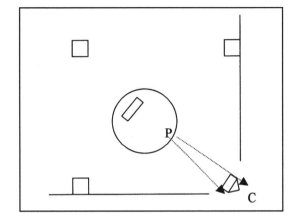

## COACH

- Talk through the purpose of the drill with the pitchers and catchers prior to the start of the drill.

- Pair up pitchers and catchers standing 45 feet apart with one baseball and a home plate. This closer distance will help the pitchers control where the ball is being located.

- The catchers will be in full gear setting up behind the plate in different locations, either inside for a few pitches or outside for a few. Different levels, high or low, can also be incorporated into the drill.

- Pitchers will throw half to three-quarter speed, working from either the windup or stretch position. Different types of pitches can be incorporated into the drill as well.

- Pitchers should throw 25 pitches during this drill. Monitor the pitcher's mechanics, providing corrections and encouragement when needed.

## PLAYER

- Pair up with a catcher with one baseball, a home plate and standing 45 feet apart.

- The catcher will be in full gear setting up in different locations, inside-outside or high-low.

- Start from the windup or the stretch position, concentrating on spotting the ball. Throw 25 pitches half to three-quarter speed, mixing in different types of pitches to spots.

# 110. Situational Pitching

**Primary Skill:** Pitching

**Objective:** To practice throwing different types of pitches to different locations and from the windup or stretch, all being dictated by the situation.

**Equipment Needed:** A baseball, catcher's gear and home plate

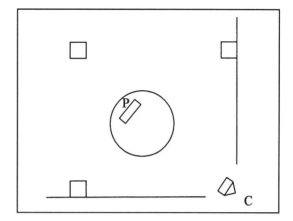

## COACH

• Explain the purpose of the drill prior to the start.

• Pair up pitchers and catchers with one ball and a home plate. The pitcher can stand at a normal distance or throw from a shorter distance.

• The catcher will give the pitcher a situation before each pitch, such as the number of outs, the count and the number of men on base, etc. The situation will dictate the location, the type of pitch and the type of motion the pitcher will use.

• The pitcher and the catcher should be working together on calling the pitches and location. Have the pitchers throw 25 to 30 pitches half to full speed depending on the time of the season and the distance from the catcher.

## PLAYER

• Pair up with a catcher with one baseball and a home plate, standing at a normal pitching distance or throwing from a shorter distance.

• The catcher will give the pitcher a situation before each pitch, such as the number of outs, the count and the number of men on base, etc. The situation will dictate the location, the type of pitch and the type of motion the pitcher will use.

• Work together with the catcher on calling the pitches and location. Throw 25 to 30 pitches half to full speed depending on the time of the season and the distance from the catcher.

# 111. Wall Drill

**Primary Skill:** Arm motion

**Objective:** To practice the backward reach of the pitcher during the pitching motion.

**Equipment Needed:** A baseball, glove and a wall

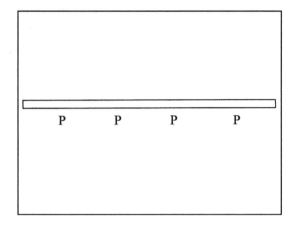

## COACH

- Explain the purpose of the drill to the pitchers before beginning.

- Align the pitchers along the wall, keeping 8 feet of space in between. The pitchers should be standing with their backs against the wall starting in the balance position.

- From there, the hands will break as their front foot is reaching toward home plate. As the throwing arm swings to the throwing position, the wall will keep the arm moving straight without it wrapping behind the body.

- Control the drill by having the pitchers perform the repetitions at the same time or one at a time to better monitor the mechanics.

- Monitor the mechanics closely as the pitchers perform the repetitions.

## PLAYER

- Align with your back against a wall, starting in a balanced position and keeping 8 feet of space between you and the next pitcher.

- Break your hands to start the throwing motion as your front foot is striding toward home plate. As the throwing arm swings to the throwing position, the wall will keep your arm moving straight without it wrapping behind your body.

- Finish the repetition by completing the throwing motion with the follow-through.

- Listen for the coach's instruction regarding the number of repetitions and the start of each repetition.

© 2001 by Prentice Hall

# 112. Hand-Break Drill

**Primary Skill:** Pitching motion

**Objective:** To reinforce and coordinate the hand break with the stride to home, keeping the body together during the pitching motion.

**Equipment Needed:** Glove and one baseball

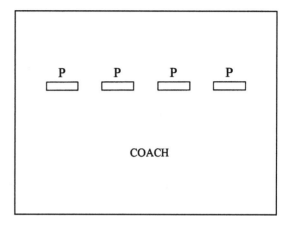

## COACH

- Explain the purpose of the drill to the players prior to the start of the drill.

- Set the pitchers in a line shoulder-to-shoulder about 6 feet apart. All pitchers will start the drill from the balance position.

- Cue the pitchers to begin the drill by breaking their hands to go to the throwing position. As the hands break, the front leg should begin striding toward home plate. The front leg should stay closed until the last possible second.

- Repeat the repetition controlling and monitoring the drill closely.

## PLAYER

- Line up shoulder-to-shoulder with about 6 feet of space in between the next pitcher facing the coach.

- Begin the drill by starting from the balance position, with the knee tucked and the foot hanging toward the ground. On the coach's cue, break your hands and begin the stride toward home plate at the same time. Do not open your front side until the last possible second.

- Reset after the repetition waiting for the coach's instructions for the start of the next repetition.

# 113. Chair Drill

**Primary Skill:** Follow-through

**Objective:** To reinforce the follow-through by the pitcher during the pitching motion.

**Equipment Needed:** Chair, glove and one baseball

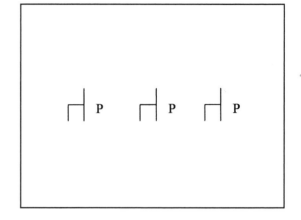

## COACH

- Demonstrate the technique to the players prior to the start of the drill.
- Each pitcher should be paired with a regular classroom chair. Use chairs that have low backs.
- The pitcher will start the drill with the back leg on the back of the chair facing home plate and the ball in the throwing hand just before the release point.
- The throwing motion should be finished with a good follow-through and the leg comes off the chair parallel to the front foot.
- Monitor the players' mechanics throughout the drill.

## PLAYER

- Pair up with a chair, starting with your back leg on the chair and throwing arm in position just before the release point of the ball.
- On the coach's signal, finish the pitching motion with your throwing arm and bring your back leg off the chair, placing it parallel to the front foot.

# SECTION 4

# CATCHING

*Success is a journey, not a destination.*

—BEN SWEETLAND

# 114. Blocking Drill—No Hands

**Primary Skill:** Blocking technique

**Objective:** To develop and reinforce the proper blocking technique without using hands when the ball is thrown in the dirt.

**Equipment Needed:** Catcher's equipment, four baseballs or tennis balls for each pair and home plates

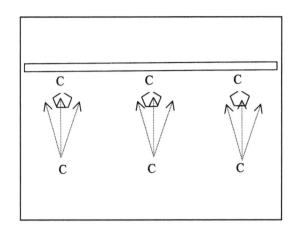

## COACH

- Set up in the gym or on the field. Demonstrate the proper technique prior to the start of the drill.
- Use home plates during the drill backed up by a screen or backstop.
- It is more efficient if multiple catchers are used. One will execute the repetitions as the catcher, while another one throws the balls.
- Make sure all catchers are equipped properly and wearing cups.
- Initially, use tennis or rag balls, especially for the younger players. Work up to the use of regular baseballs.
- Emphasize blocking balls in the dirt instead of trying to catch them. By not using hands, the catchers will learn the concept of using the body to keep the ball in front.
- Monitor the drill closely, offering continuous encouragement.

## PLAYER

- Pair up with another catcher and put on the full catcher's gear. Keep your hands behind your back, while another catcher becomes the thrower.
- The throwers stand approximately 15 feet in front of the plate, bouncing balls in front of the catcher. Allow your partner to reset in a catcher' stance between throws.
- Block the thrown balls using the proper technique; do not attempt to catch the ball, just block it.
- Switch after at least 10 repetitions.

**NOTE:** Use the drill during pregame as part of the catcher warm-ups and to reinforce the proper technique.

# 115. Blocking Drill—Ball in Front

**Primary Skill:** Blocking technique

**Objective:** To develop and reinforce the proper blocking technique when the ball is thrown in the dirt in front of the catcher.

**Equipment Needed:** Catcher's equipment, four baseballs or tennis balls for each pair and home plates

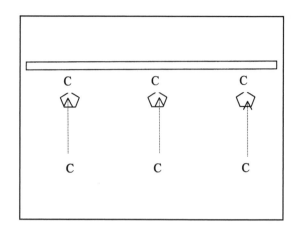

## COACH

- Set up in the gym or on the field. Demonstrate the proper technique prior to the start of the drill.
- Use home plates against a screen or backstop for the drill.
- It is more efficient if multiple catchers are used. Pair the catchers, one throwing the balls while the other blocks, then switch.
- Make sure all the catchers are equipped properly and wearing cups.
- Initially use tennis or rag balls, especially for the younger players. Work up to the use of regular baseballs.
- Emphasize blocking balls in the dirt instead of trying to catch them.
- Monitor the drill closely, offering continuous encouragement.

## PLAYER

- Pair up with another catcher and put on the full catcher's gear, with your partner as the thrower.
- The throwers stand approximately 15 feet in front of the plate and throw balls in the dirt in front of the catcher. Allow your partner to reset in a good catcher's stance between throws.
- Block the thrown balls using the proper technique; do not attempt to catch the ball, just block it.
- Switch after at least 10 repetitions.

**NOTE:** Use the drill during pregame as part of the catcher warm-ups and to reinforce the proper technique.

# 116. Blocking Drill—Balls to the Left or Right

**Primary Skill:** Blocking technique

**Objective:** To develop and reinforce the proper blocking technique when the ball is thrown in the dirt to the left or to the right of the catcher.

**Equipment Needed:** Catcher's equipment, four baseballs or tennis balls for each pair and home plates

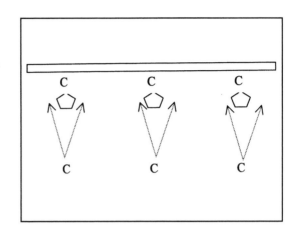

## COACH

- Set up in the gym or on the field. Demonstrate the proper technique prior to the start of the drill.
- Use home plates against a screen or backstop for the drill.
- It is more efficient if multiple catchers are used. Pair catchers, one throwing the balls while the other blocks, then switch.
- Make sure all the catchers are equipped properly and wearing cups.
- Initially use tennis or rag balls, especially for the younger players. Work up to the use of regular baseballs.
- Emphasize blocking balls in the dirt instead of catching them.
- Monitor the drill closely, offering continuous encouragement.

## PLAYER

- Pair up with another catcher and put on full catcher's gear, while your partner serves as the thrower.
- The throwers stand approximately 15 feet in front of the plate, throwing balls to the left and to the right of the catcher. Allow your partner to reset in the catcher's stance between throws.
- Block the thrown balls using the proper technique; do not attempt to catch the ball, just block it.
- Switch after at least 10 repetitions.

**NOTE:** Use the drill during pregame as part of catcher warm-ups and to reinforce the proper technique.

# 117. Blocking Drill—Throwing to Bases

**Primary Skill:** Blocking and throwing techniques

**Objective:** To develop and reinforce the proper blocking technique when the ball is in the dirt and a throw to a base is required.

**Equipment Needed:** Catcher's equipment, four baseballs or tennis balls for each pair and home plates

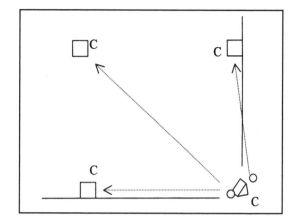

## COACH

- Set up in the gym or on the field. Demonstrate the proper technique prior to the start of the drill.
- Use home plates against a screen or backstop for the drill.
- It is more efficient if multiple catchers are used. One will execute the repetitions as the catcher, while another throws the balls and another covers a base.
- Make sure all the catchers are equipped properly and wearing cups.
- Initially use tennis or rag balls, especially for the younger players. Work up to the use of regular baseballs.
- Emphasize blocking the balls in the dirt instead of catching them.
- Monitor the drill closely, offering continuous encouragement.

## PLAYER

- Pair up with another catcher and put on full catcher's gear, while another catcher becomes a thrower and another catcher covers a base.
- The throwers stand approximately 15 feet in front of the plate, throwing balls to the left, in front and to the right. After the ball is blocked, move to the ball and throw to the designated base. Allow your partner to reset in the catcher's stance between throws.
- Block the thrown balls using the proper technique; do not attempt to catch the ball, just block it.
- Switch after at least 10 repetitions.

**NOTE:** Use the drill during pregame as part of catcher warm-ups and to reinforce the proper technique.

# 118. Release Drill

**Primary Skill:** Movement to release point

**Objective:** To develop and reinforce the catcher's stance to allow releasing the ball with quickness.

**Equipment Needed:** Two or three baseballs per pair and catcher's equipment

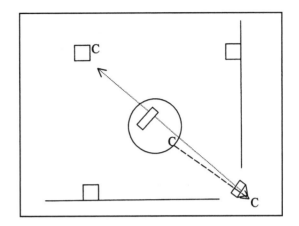

## COACH

- Set up in the gym or on the field. Demonstrate the movement prior to the start of the drill.
- Pair the catchers, with one in full gear and the other tossing balls from the front of the pitcher's mound.
- Monitor the catcher's stance prior to the tossing and then the release motion.
- Initially have the catchers perform the movement to the release position, then move to releasing or throwing the ball. Use another catcher to receive the throws.

## PLAYER

- Pair up with another catcher in full gear.
- One player stands in front of the pitcher's mound tossing the ball to the catcher in full gear.
- The catcher starts in a stance with the runner on base, catching the ball and moving to the throwing position and release point. Eventually the balls will be thrown to second base.

# 119. Foul Ball

**Primary Skill:** Fielding foul balls

**Objective:** To develop and reinforce the proper technique for fielding foul pop-ups behind home plate.

**Equipment Needed:** Home plate, catcher's gear and three or four baseballs

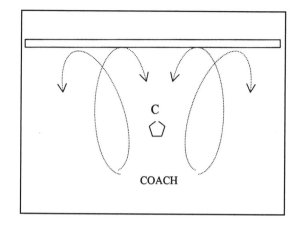

## COACH

• Set up either in the gym or on the field, although it is more beneficial outside on the field.

• Use one catcher at a time with at least head gear. Full gear may be used—get the catchers used to moving in full gear.

• Demonstrate the proper technique prior to the drill. Immediately face the backstop, trying to keep the ball slightly in front of the body. Hold the mask in hand until the ball is spotted, then toss the mask out of the way to ensure you can make a catch without tripping over the errant mask.

• Throw the balls in the air behind the catcher, high enough to give the catcher time to position.

• Provide constant encouragement during the drill.

## PLAYER

• Use at least a mask and helmet, but use full gear if available.

• Start from a catcher's stance. When the coach throws the ball, react to the foul by using the proper technique. Check above for technique reminders.

**NOTE:** Catchers need to practice this drill throughout the season.

# 120. Throws to First Base

**Primary Skill:** Throwing the ball to a base

**Objective:** To reinforce and practice throws to first base from behind the plate.

**Equipment Needed:** Six baseballs, home plate, catcher's gear and a base

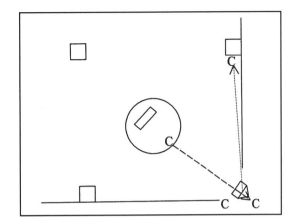

## COACH

- Set up in the gym or on the field. If in the gym, measure the distance from home to first base.
- One catcher is in full gear, another representing a right-handed batter and another covering the first base bag.
- Stand in front of the pitcher's mound to throw pitches, making sure the pitches can be handled easily by the catcher.
- Monitor the catcher's man on base stance and provide constant encouragement throughout the drill.

## PLAYER

- Put on the catcher's gear to take repetitions behind the plate. While waiting to take repetitions behind the plate, either take a right-handed batter's position or cover the first base bag.
- Start from a man-on-base ready stance, waiting for the coach's throw. Receive the ball and then make a throw to the first base bag.
- Rotate through the drill to cover each position, catcher, batter and the first base bag.

**NOTE:** Set the catcher slightly deeper (by a half step) to clear the batter when making a throw to first base.

# 121. Throws to Third Base

**Primary Skill:** Throwing the ball to a base

**Objective:** To reinforce and practice throws to third base from behind the plate.

**Equipment Needed:** Six baseballs, home plate, catcher's gear and a base

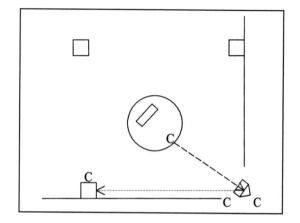

## COACH

- Set up in the gym or on the field. If in the gym, measure the distance from home to third base.

- One catcher is in full gear, another representing a right-handed batter and a third covering the third base bag.

- Stand in front of the pitcher's mound to throw pitches, making sure the pitches can be handled easily by the catcher.

- Monitor the catcher's man on base stance and provide constant encouragement throughout the drill.

## PLAYER

- Put on catcher's gear to take repetitions behind the plate. While waiting to take repetitions behind the plate, either take a right-handed batter's position or cover third base.

- Start from a man-on-base ready stance, waiting for the coach's throw. Receive the ball and then make a throw to third base.

- Rotate through the drill to cover each position, catcher, batter and the third base bag.

**NOTE:** Set the catcher slightly deeper (a half step) to clear the batter when making a throw to third base.

# 122. Fielding Bunts

**Primary Skill:** Fielding bunts

**Objective:** To reinforce and
practice the catcher's ability to
field a bunted ball.

**Equipment Needed:** Home plates,
three baseballs per group and
catcher's gear

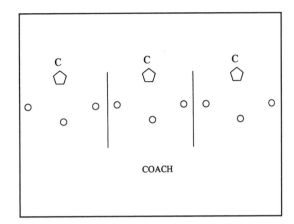

## COACH

- Set up in the gym or on the field with the catchers.

- Talk through and demonstrate the proper mechanics.

- Set up three home plates with three catchers. Place the balls in three different locations 5 to 6 feet in front of the plate. Perform this drill without throws to the bases—check for positioning.

- Monitor the drill closely, providing corrections and encouragement when needed.

## PLAYER

- Execute the drill with or without gear.

- Always start from a catcher's stance behind home plate; wait for the coach's cue to move.

- Move toward the ball, with the non-throwing shoulder toward the target, and scoop the ball with the hand and glove together. Avoid fielding the ball with only the glove.

- Once the ball is fielded, continue to move toward the target. Take three repetitions and then rotate with the other catchers.

# 123. Fielding Bunts—Throwing to First Base

**Primary Skill:** Fielding bunts

**Objective:** To reinforce and practice fielding a bunted ball and then throwing to first base.

**Equipment Needed:** Home plates, three baseballs, catcher's gear and a base

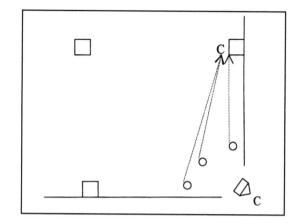

## COACH

- Set up in the gym or on the field with the catchers.

- Talk through and demonstrate the proper mechanics.

- Set up a home plate with one catcher and use another catcher to take the throws at first base. Place the balls in three different locations 5 to 6 feet in front of the plate. The catcher should get into a good stance and move toward one of the balls, field it and throw to first base.

- Give each catcher three repetitions. Monitor the catcher's mechanics during the drill.

## PLAYER

- Execute drill with or without gear.

- Always start from a stance behind home plate; wait for the coach's cue to move.

- Move toward the ball, with the non-throwing shoulder toward the target, and scoop the ball with the hand and glove together. Avoid fielding the ball with only your glove.

- Once the ball is fielded, continue to move toward first base and make the throw. Take three repetitions and then rotate with the other catchers.

# 124. Fielding Bunts—Throwing to Second Base

**Primary Skill:** Fielding bunts

**Objective:** To reinforce and practice fielding a bunted ball and then throwing to second base.

**Equipment Needed:** Home plates, three baseballs, catcher's gear and a base

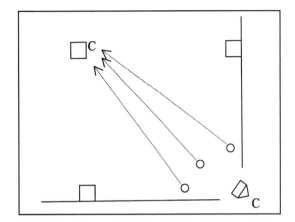

## COACH

• Set up in the gym or on the field with catchers.

• Talk through and demonstrate the proper mechanics.

• Set up a home plate with one catcher in normal position and another catcher prepared to take the throws at second base. Place the balls in three different locations 5 to 6 feet in front of the plate. The catcher should get into a good stance, then move toward one of the balls, field it and throw to second base.

• Give each catcher three repetitions. Monitor the catcher's mechanics during the drill.

## PLAYER

• Execute drill with or without gear.

• Always start from a stance behind home plate; wait for the coach's cue to move.

• Move toward the ball, with the non-throwing shoulder toward the target, and scoop the ball with the hand and glove together. Avoid fielding the ball with only your glove.

• Once the ball is fielded, continue to move toward second base and make the throw. Take three repetitions and then rotate with the other catchers.

# 125. Fielding Bunts—Throwing to Third Base

**Primary Skill:** Fielding bunts

**Objective:** To reinforce and practice fielding a bunted ball and then throwing to third base.

**Equipment Needed:** Home plates, three baseballs, catcher's gear and a base

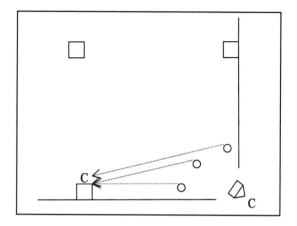

## COACH

- Set up with catchers in the gym or on the field.

- Talk through and demonstrate the proper mechanics.

- Set up a home plate with one catcher behind the plate and another catcher taking the throws at third base. Place the balls in three different locations 5 to 6 feet in front of the plate. The catcher should get into a good stance, then move toward one of the balls, field it and throw to third base.

- Give each catcher three repetitions. Monitor the catcher's mechanics during the drill.

## PLAYER

- Execute the drill with or without gear.

- Always start from a stance behind home plate; wait for the coach's cue to move.

- Move toward the ball, with the non-throwing shoulder toward the target, and scoop the ball with the hand and glove together. Avoid fielding the ball with only your glove.

- Once ball is fielded, continue to move toward third base and make the throw. Take three repetitions and then rotate with the other catchers.

# 126. Setup Drill—Classroom

**Primary Skill:** Stance

**Objective:** To reinforce the proper stance of the catcher during the game.

**Equipment Needed:** Catcher's gear and a home plate

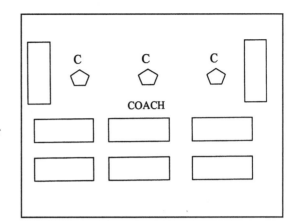

## COACH

- Demonstrate the proper technique prior to the start of the drill.

- Clear an area in the classroom so that three catchers can set up in a good stance side by side about 3 feet apart.

- Start the catchers in a relaxed position, giving a cue to get into a good stance. Have all the catchers get into a stance at the same time.

- Check for the proper body position: feet at shoulder width, toes straight ahead, knees straight ahead, butt low and back leaning slightly forward.

- Monitor the stances while catchers hold this position.

## PLAYER

- Line up shoulder-to-shoulder in a straight line about 3 feet apart.

- Face the coach in a relaxed position waiting for a cue to get into a good stance.

- Once in the stance, remember good body position with feet at shoulder width, toes pointed straight ahead, knees straight ahead, butt low and your back leaning slightly forward.

- Hold this position while the coach checks for proper body position.

# 127. Setup Drill

**Primary Skill:** Stance

**Objective:** To reinforce the proper stance of the catcher during the game.

**Equipment Needed:** Catcher's gear and a home plate

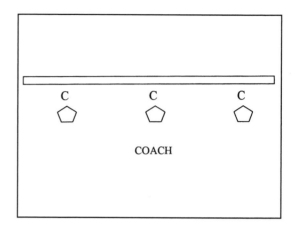

## COACH

- Demonstrate the proper technique prior to the start of the drill.
- Line up catchers shoulder-to-shoulder in a straight line about 6 feet apart without gear initially.
- Start catchers in a relaxed position, giving a cue to get into a good stance. Have all catchers get into a stance at the same time.
- Check for proper body position: feet at shoulder width, toes straight ahead, knees straight ahead, butt low and back leaning slightly forward.
- Monitor stances while catchers hold the position.

## PLAYER

- Line up shoulder-to-shoulder in a straight line about 6 feet apart without catcher's gear initially.
- Face the coach in a relaxed position waiting for a cue to get into a good stance.
- Once in the stance, remember good body position with feet at shoulder width, toes pointed straight ahead, knees straight ahead, butt low and your back leaning slightly forward.
- Hold this position while the coach checks for the proper body position.

# 128. Signal Drill

**Primary Skill:** Giving signals

**Objective:** To practice giving signals so they can be seen only by the pitcher.

**Equipment Needed:** Catcher's gear and a home plate

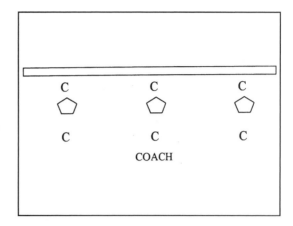

## COACH

- Demonstrate the proper technique prior to the start of the drill.

- Line up catchers shoulder-to-shoulder in a straight line about 6 feet apart, paired up, without gear initially.

- Start the catchers in a relaxed position giving a cue to get into a good stance. Have one set of catchers get into a stance.

- Once the catchers are in a stance, have them give signals to their partner. Monitor their stance and signals to see if signals are hidden.

## PLAYER

- Pair up with another catcher in a straight line about 15 feet apart, without catcher's gear initially.

- Face the coach in a relaxed position, waiting for a cue to get into a good stance.

- Once in the stance, remember good body position with feet at shoulder width, toes pointed straight ahead, knees straight ahead, butt low and your back leaning slightly forward.

- Give your partner signals using good technique to hide the signals. After about five repetitions, your partner will give the signals.

# 129. Throwing Drill

**Primary Skill:** Throwing

**Objective:** To practice gripping the ball properly while throwing.

**Equipment Needed:** A baseball per pair and gloves

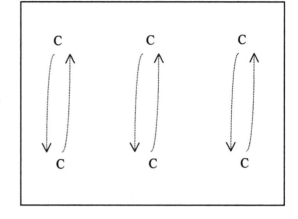

## COACH

- Demonstrate the proper mechanics prior to the start of the drill.
- Pair up catchers standing about 30 feet apart with one baseball.
- One catcher will throw to the other; when the ball is received, the catcher needs to quickly try to grip the ball across the seams before making a throw.
- The catchers should take 15 to 20 throws, trying to increase quickness when gripping the ball.
- Monitor the drill closely, checking the catchers' grips from time to time.

## PLAYER

- Pair up with another catcher standing about 30 feet apart with a baseball.
- Before throwing to your partner, quickly grip the ball across the seams while it is in the glove, then throw the ball to your partner.
- When your partner receives the ball, the same routine needs to be performed. Take 15 to 20 throws, trying to increase quickness when gripping the ball on each throw.

# 130. Backup Drill—Third Base

**Primary Skill:** Backing up third base

**Objective:** To practice backing up third base during a bunt situation when the third baseman fields the ball with a runner on first base.

**Equipment Needed:** Catcher's gear, six baseballs and a base

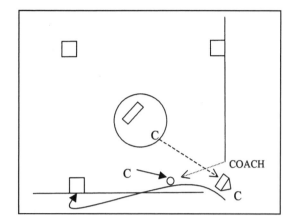

## COACH

- Talk through the purpose prior to the start of the drill.

- Place a catcher behind home plate in a good stance with another catcher playing the third base position. Place another catcher in front of the pitcher's mound to throw pitches to the catcher.

- Place a ball down the third base line to simulate a bunted ball so the third baseman, the pitcher or the catcher has to field the ball.

- After the pitch to the catcher, the catcher and the third baseman break for the ball. If the third baseman fields the ball, the catcher moves to cover third base.

- Rotate catchers after three repetitions. Monitor the drill closely.

## PLAYER

- Align in catcher's gear in a good stance behind the plate. Another catcher plays third base, while another catcher stands in front of the mound to throw pitches to the catcher.

- Wait for the pitch, then break to the ball lying along the third base line. If the third baseman fields the ball, move toward the third base bag for coverage.

- Take three repetitions before rotating to other positions.

# 131. Backup Drill—First Base

**Primary Skill:** Backing up first base

**Objective:** To practice backing up first base on a ball thrown to first base with no runner on base.

**Equipment Needed:** Catcher's gear, six baseballs and a base

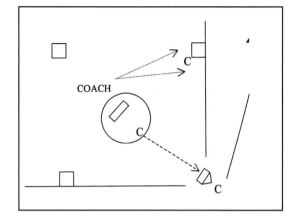

## COACH

- Explain the purpose prior to the start of the drill.

- Place the catchers in a good stance at home plate. Another catcher plays first base to take throws, while another stands in front of the pitcher's mound to throw pitches to the catcher.

- After the pitch, the catcher will break toward first base to a backup position 15 to 20 feet behind the first base bag.

- Stand behind the mound to throw balls to first base; make good throws and bad throws.

- Each catcher should take three repetitions before rotating to other positions. Monitor each repetition closely.

## PLAYER

- Align in catcher's gear in a good stance behind the plate. Another catcher plays the first base position, while another catcher stands in front of the mound to throw pitches to the catcher.

- After a pitch is thrown, break toward first base to back up throw being made by the coach. The backup position should be 15 to 20 feet behind the first base bag.

- Take three repetitions before rotating to the other positions.

# 132. Tag Drill

**Primary Skill:** Blocking and tagging

**Objective:** To practice blocking home plate and making the tag on a runner attempting to score.

**Equipment Needed:** Catcher's gear, six baseballs and a home plate

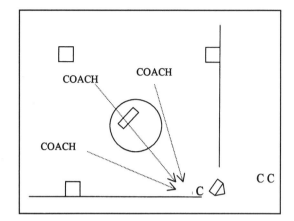

## COACH

• Explain and demonstrate the proper technique prior to the start of the drill.

• Place the catchers at home plate, one taking repetitions at a time.

• Stand at different spots in the infield to throw balls to the catcher. This is to make the catcher position for throws from different angles from the outfield.

• Have the catcher make a play on the ball, then get into position to block the plate and make the tag.

• Rotate catchers after a few repetitions, monitor repetitions closely.

## PLAYER

• Align at home plate in full gear waiting for balls hit or thrown by the coach from different angles in the infield.

• Once the ball is thrown, play the ball, get into a blocking position and make a tag on the runner.

• Take a few repetitions before rotating with the other catchers.

# 133. Third Strike Drill

**Primary Skill:** Playing dropped third strike

**Objective:** To practice having the catcher react to a dropped third strike by either tagging the batter or throwing the ball to first base.

**Equipment Needed:** Catcher's gear, six baseballs, home plate and a base

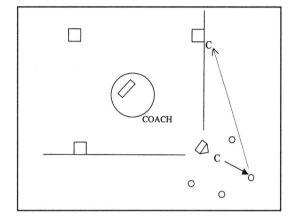

## COACH

- Demonstrate the proper technique prior to the start of the drill.

- Place one catcher in full gear at home plate and another catcher at first base to take throws.

- Place balls around the home plate area, either in front, behind or to the sides. Start the drill by having the catcher in a good stance behind home plate.

- On the coach's signal the catcher will break for one of the balls around the home plate area. Once the ball is retrieved, the catcher makes an inside or outside call to the first baseman to tell which side of the runner the ball will be thrown from just before throw is made.

- Repeat repetitions two or three times before rotating the catchers.

## PLAYER

- Align at home plate in full gear with another catcher at first base to take throws.

- Wait for the coach's signal to break for one of the balls lying around the home plate area. Once the ball is retrieved, communicate with the first baseman whether the throw will be inside or outside, then make the throw.

- Take two or three repetitions before rotating.

# 134. Wide Pitch Drill

**Primary Skill:** Movement on wide pitch

**Objective:** To practice stepping out to receive a pitch wide out of the strike zone.

**Equipment Needed:** Catcher's gear, six baseballs and a home plate

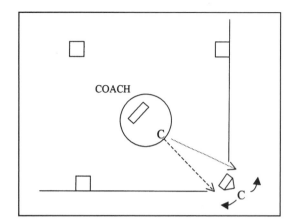

## COACH

- Demonstrate the proper technique prior to the start of the drill.

- Pair the catchers with each pair having a home plate and three baseballs. One catcher sets behind home plate in a good stance in full gear, while the other stands about 30 feet away throwing pitches wide of the strike zone to either side.

- The catcher receiving the pitches uses good technique to get to the wide pitches by stepping out with the near foot.

- Monitor the catchers' mechanics closely and rotate the catchers after five repetitions.

## PLAYER

- Pair up with another catcher. Get into a good stance in full gear behind home plate, while the other catcher stands 30 feet away throwing wide pitches.

- Use good technique to move toward the wide pitch by stepping with the near foot.

- Take five repetitions before rotating with your partner.

# 135. Bases Loaded Drill

**Primary Skill:** Footwork on force play

**Objective:** To practice and reinforce footwork by the catcher at home plate when bases are loaded.

**Equipment Needed:** Catcher's gear, six baseballs, home plate and a base

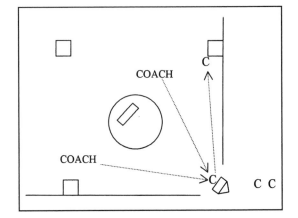

## COACH

- Explain the purpose and demonstrate the proper technique prior to the start of the drill.

- Place the catchers at home plate in full gear and one catcher at first base.

- Stand approximately 30 feet away from the catcher to make throws to home plate. Start the catcher behind the plate in a good stance. Give the catcher a signal to move to the front of the plate waiting for a throw for a force-out.

- The catcher's right foot should be on the plate for the force-out; as soon as the ball is caught, a throw is then made to first base.

- Rotate the catchers every two or three repetitions and monitor the catchers' technique, closely providing encouragement during the drill.

## PLAY

- Align behind home plate in full gear in a good stance, while another catcher is placed at first base for throws.

- Watch for the coach's signal to move in front of the plate to receive a throw. Receive the throw with right foot on the plate for the force-out, then step toward first base to make a throw.

- Take two or three repetitions before rotating with the catcher playing the first base bag.

# 136. Pop-Up Drill

**Primary Skill:** Catching pop-ups

**Objective:** To practice catching pop-ups.

**Equipment Needed:** Catcher's gear, six baseballs and a home plate

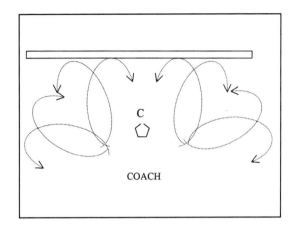

## COACH

- Explain the purpose and demonstrate the proper technique prior to the start of the drill.
- Place the catchers at home plate in full gear starting in a good stance. From that position throw or hit a pop-up to the catcher.
- Remind the catchers to face the backstop when attempting to catch the ball, as well as holding onto the mask until the ball is located in the air.
- Give each catcher two or three repetitions before switching. Monitor mechanics closely, making corrections as well as providing encouragement.

## PLAYER

- Align behind home plate in full gear in a good stance, waiting for the coach to hit a pop-up.
- Once the ball is in the air, remove your mask, face the backstop and keep the ball slightly in front of you. When the ball is located, toss the catcher's mask to the side and get your body in position to catch the ball.
- Take two or three repetitions before switching.

# 137. Passed Ball Drill

**Primary Skill:** Retrieving a passed ball

**Objective:** To practice and reinforce retrieving a ball that has gotten past the catcher, then tossing the ball to the pitcher covering home plate.

**Equipment Needed:** Catcher's gear, glove, home plate and six baseballs

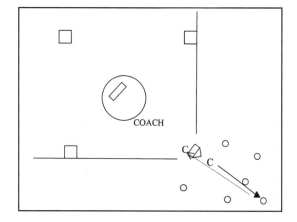

## COACH

- Explain the purpose and demonstrate the proper technique prior to the start of the drill.
- Place one catcher in full gear behind the plate with baseballs in different locations near the backstop.
- Another catcher will cover home plate when the catcher behind the plate breaks for one of the balls located near the backstop.
- Have the catchers take two or three repetitions before rotating. Monitor mechanics closely throughout the drill.

## PLAYER

- Set up behind home plate in full gear in a good stance. Another catcher will cover home plate to take the throws.
- From the set position, break to retrieve one of the passed balls near the backstop. Once the ball is retrieved, make a quick but accurate toss to the player covering home plate.
- Take two or three repetitions before rotating with the other catchers.

© 2001 by Prentice Hall

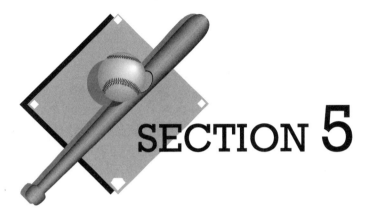

# SECTION 5

# COMBINATION DRILLS

*To be a winner, all you need to give is all you have.*

—ANONYMOUS

# 138. Pitcher/First Base Coverage

**Primary Skill:** Pitcher covering first base, first baseman tossing ball to pitcher covering first base

**Objective:** To develop and reinforce the proper technique for the pitcher covering first base; the proper presentation and throwing of the ball by the first baseman to the pitcher covering the bag.

**Equipment Needed:** Four baseballs, first base, pitching rubber and a fungo bat

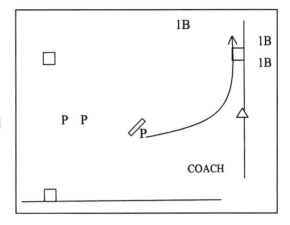

## COACH

- Set up the drill by demonstrating to both the pitcher and the first baseman the proper technique.
- Place a cone along the first base line as a target for pitchers, 10 to 12 feet from first base.
- Place the pitchers at the pitcher's mound and the first baseman at the first base bag.
- Start the drill without the ball to practice fielding positions and movements and then throw or hit ground balls to the first baseman for live repetitions.
- Constantly monitor techniques during repetitions, providing encouragement.

## PLAYER

- Align in normal positions at the pitcher's mound and at first base, waiting for the coach to throw or hit a ground ball.
- Pitcher: start with the windup or stretch motion; when a ground ball is thrown or hit, move toward first base quickly, aiming for a spot approximately 10 to 12 feet toward the homeplate side of the first baseline. Bend your path to square your shoulders toward first base with your hands in a receiving position. If you reach first base before the throw, play the bag as a first baseman.
- First baseman: field the ball at first base, then remove it from your glove with a bare hand, make an overhand or underhand throw to the pitcher, chest high.

**NOTE:** The first baseman must field the ball first and then give the pitcher a toss that is clearly in view and can be handled.

# 139. Fly Ball Communication—Left Fielder, Third Baseman and Shortstop

**Primary Skill:** Communication

**Objective:** To practice communication between the left fielder, third baseman and shortstop on fly balls, while reinforcing fielding techniques for each position.

**Equipment Needed:** Six baseballs, gloves and a fungo bat

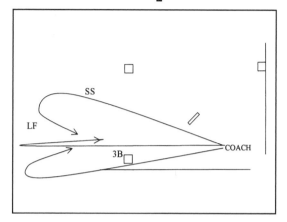

## COACH

- Begin demonstrating the proper technique for both the infield and the outfield positions, stressing communication. Remind the players that the outfielders have the right-of-way on any ball that they can catch.
- Set up the drill in shallow left field. Throw or hit the ball from the shortstop area on the infield grass to shallow left field, having the three positions converge on the ball. Remember throwing the ball provides more control to the drill.
- Monitor the fielders' technique while moving toward the ball and the communication during the drill.

## PLAYER

- Align in the proper position at third base, shortstop and left field.
- Get into a good ready position, waiting for the ball to be thrown or hit by the coach to shallow left field.
- Infielders: break toward the fly ball with the intent to make the catch, continue toward the ball until the outfielder makes the call or the catch.
- Outfielders: break toward the ball with the intent to make the catch; if the catch can be made, communicate with the infielders immediately.
- As soon as the catch is made, gather your feet to make a throw, then rotate to the back of the line.

**NOTE:** The outfielders have the right-of-way, but still need to communicate.

# 140. Fly Ball Communication—Center Fielder, Shortstop and Second Baseman

**Primary Skill:** Communication

**Objective:** To practice communication between the center fielder, second baseman and shortstop on fly balls, while reinforcing fielding techniques for each position.

**Equipment Needed:** Six baseballs, gloves and a fungo bat

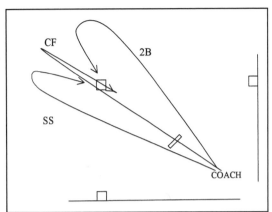

## COACH

- Begin by demonstrating the proper technique for both the infield and the outfield positions, stressing communication. Remind the players that the outfielders have the right-of-way on any ball they can catch.
- Set up the drill in the shallow center field area. Throw or hit the ball from behind the pitcher's mound on the infield grass to shallow center field, having the three positions converge on the ball. Remember throwing the ball provides more control to the drill.
- Monitor the fielders' technique while moving toward the ball and the communication during the drill.

## PLAYER

- Align in the proper position at second base, shortstop and center field.
- Get into a good ready position, waiting for the ball to be thrown or hit by the coach into shallow center field.
- Infielders: break toward the fly ball with the intent to make the catch, continue toward the ball until the outfielder makes a call or a catch.
- Outfielders: break toward ball with the intent to make the catch; if the catch can be made, communicate with the infielders immediately.
- As soon as the catch is made, gather your feet to make a throw, then rotate to the back of the line.

**NOTE:** The outfielders have the right-of-way, but still need to communicate.

# 141. Fly Ball Communication—Right Fielder, First Baseman and Second Baseman

**Primary Skill:** Communication

**Objective:** To practice communication between the right fielder, first baseman and second baseman on fly balls, while reinforcing fielding techniques for each position.

**Equipment Needed:** Six baseballs, gloves and a fungo bat

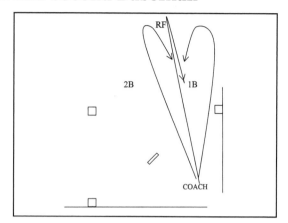

## COACH

- Begin demonstrating the proper technique for both the infield and the outfield positions, stressing communication. Remind the players that the outfielders have the right-of-way on any ball they can catch.
- Set up the drill in the shallow right field area. Throw or hit the ball from the second base area on the infield grass to shallow right field, having the three positions converge on the ball. Remember throwing the ball provides more control to the drill.
- Monitor the fielders' technique while moving toward the ball and the communication during the drill.

## PLAYER

- Align in the proper position at first base, second base and right field.
- Get into a good ready position, waiting for the ball to be thrown or hit by the coach to shallow right field.
- Infielders: break toward the fly ball with the intent to make the catch, continue toward the ball until the outfielder makes a call or a catch.
- Outfielders: break toward the ball with the intent to make the catch; if the catch can be made, communicate with the infielders immediately.
- As soon as the catch is made, gather your feet to make a throw, then rotate to the back of the line.

**NOTE:** The outfielders have the right-of-way, but still need to communicate.

# 142. Home Plate Coverage

**Primary Skill:** Home plate coverage, ball retrieval

**Objective:** To practice pitcher and catcher communication and coverage of home plate during a passed ball or wild pitch situation.

**Equipment Needed:** Three baseballs, full catcher's gear, home plate and a pitching rubber

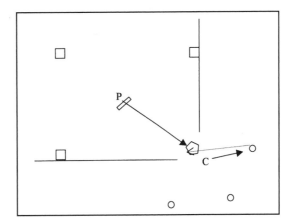

## COACH

- Set up the drill by placing balls in three different locations behind the catcher: one directly behind the catcher at the backstop, another toward first base again behind the catcher, a final one toward third base also behind the catcher.
- Place pitchers and catchers in normal positions. The pitcher performs the windup or the stretch motion. As soon as the motion is finished, the pitcher calls out the direction for the catcher.
- The pitcher covers home plate, while the catcher retrieves the ball, then tosses it to the pitcher.
- Monitor movement, technique and communication throughout the drill, providing encouragement.

## PLAYER

- Start in a normal position on the mound or behind home plate.
- The pitcher goes through a motion to simulate the pitch and for timing. After the pitch is made, the pitcher makes a call to the catcher "first base" for a ball toward the first base-line, "backstop" for a ball straight back, "third base" for a ball toward the third baseline.
- When the catcher breaks for the ball, the pitcher breaks for home, then the catcher makes a flip throw to the pitcher at home plate.
- After repetition move to the back of line.

**NOTE:** Teach plate coverage to the pitchers before the drill.

# 143. Run Down Between First Base and Second Base

**Primary Skill:** Run-down rotation

**Objective:** To practice and reinforce the proper technique and positioning during a run-down situation between first and second base.

**Equipment Needed:** Two or three baseballs, gloves and bags

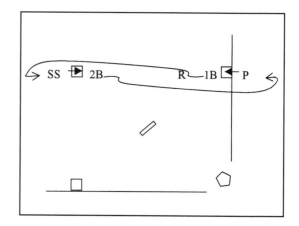

## COACH

- Demonstrate the proper rotation; use outfielders or extra infielders as runners.

- Set up the drill between first and second base, involving the first baseman, the pitcher, the second baseman and the shortstop. Walk through a few repetitions; quality repetitions are more important than quantity.

- Monitor the drill, constantly checking on the rotation.

## PLAYER

- Start the drill with a partner at first or second, using an extra player as a runner.

- Keep the ball in your throwing hand, held high, visible, cocked ready to throw, outside the baseline. Do not fake—your teammate is usually the only one fooled.

- Receive the ball with your glove outside the baseline to avoid the ball hitting the runner.

- Constrict the runner after each throw; this should take only three or four throws. Move closer after each throw, taking away running room.

- Always force the base runner back toward the starting point, the base farthest from home.

- After each throw follow the ball outside the baseline, backing up the infielder at the next base.

# 144. Run Down Between Second Base and Third Base

**Primary Skill:** Run-down rotation

**Objective:** To practice and reinforce the proper technique and positioning during a run-down situation between second and third base.

**Equipment Needed:** Two or three baseballs, gloves and bags

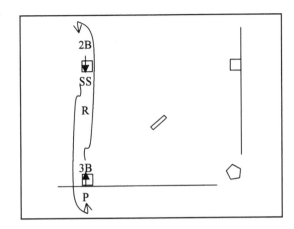

## COACH

- Demonstrate the proper rotation; use outfielders or extra infielders as runners.

- Set up the drill between second and third base, involving the second baseman, the shortstop, the third baseman and the pitcher. Walk through a few repetitions; quality repetitions are more important than quantity.

- Monitor the drill, constantly checking on the rotation.

## PLAYER

- Start the drill with a partner at second or third, using an extra player as a runner.

- Keep the ball in your throwing hand, held high, visible, cocked ready to throw, outside the baseline. Do not fake—your teammate is usually the only one fooled.

- Receive the ball with your glove outside the baseline to avoid the ball hitting the runner.

- Constrict the runner after each throw; this should take only three or four throws. Move closer after each throw, taking away running room.

- Always force the base runner back toward starting point, the base farthest from home.

- After each throw follow the ball outside the baseline, backing up the infielder at the next base.

# 145. Run Down Between Third Base and Home Plate

**Primary Skill:** Run-down rotation

**Objective:** To practice and reinforce the proper technique and positioning during a run-down situation between third base and home plate.

**Equipment Needed:** Two or three baseballs, gloves and bags

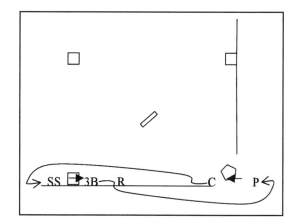

## COACH

- Demonstrate the proper rotation; use outfielders or extra infielders as runners

- Set up the drill between third base and home plate, involving the third baseman, the shortstop, the pitcher and the catcher. Walk through a few repetitions; quality repetitions are more important than quantity.

- Monitor the drill, constantly checking on the rotation.

## PLAYER

- Start the drill with a partner at third or home plate, using an extra player as a runner.

- Keep the ball in your throwing hand, held high, visible, cocked ready to throw, outside the baseline. Do not fake—your teammate is usually the only one fooled.

- Receive the ball with your glove outside the baseline to avoid the ball hitting the runner

- Constrict the runner after each throw, this should take only three or four throws. Move closer after each throw, taking away running room.

- Always force the base runner back toward third base.

- After each throw follow the ball outside the baseline, backing up the infielder at the next base.

# 146. First and Third

**Primary Skill:** Defending the first and third situation

**Objective:** To practice and develop ways to defend the first and third situation by using different options/plays.

**Equipment Needed:** Six baseballs, gloves, bases and catcher's equipment

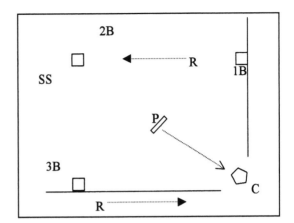

## COACH

- Set runners at first and third with the infielders in the proper alignment.

- Decide before coming onto the field which options to use. Talk and walk through the plays before running the live drill.

- Use extra infielders as runners; indicate to the runners that this is a live offensive drill as well. Use other coaches to monitor the runners.

- Rotate other players after a few repetitions.

## PLAYER

- Align in regular infield positions, waiting for a call or signal from the coach before the pitch is delivered.

- The pitcher starts off in the stretch position. The ball is either delivered home or a pick-off attempt is made.

- The runners attempt to steal every repetition, stay at first as a change-up. When the runner breaks, execute the play that was called.

- Take the number of repetitions determined by the coach before switching.

**NOTE:** This drill is a framework for each coach to use designated techniques/plays in this situation. A talk and a walk-through while teaching the plays is optimal. If these plays are going to be used throughout the season, continue to review.

# 147. Holding Runners Close—First Base

**Primary Skill:** Defending runner on base

**Objective:** To practice and reinforce holding runners close to first base, as well as proper timing during pick-off plays.

**Equipment Needed:** Three baseballs, gloves, base and catcher's equipment

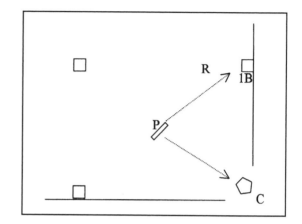

© 2001 by Prentice Hall

## COACH

- Talk through the drill prior to the start. Place the pitchers, the first basemen and the catchers in their regular positions. Either have the first baseman hold the runner on or play behind the runner in a regular alignment.
- Use extra infielders as runners; indicate to the runners that this is a live offensive drill as well. Use another coach to monitor runners.
- Remind the pitchers of the pick-off techniques, options to keep the runners close and to throw off the runner's timing.
- Rotate other players after three or four repetitions.
- Monitor infield's position before pick-off attempt and after throw to bag.

## PLAYER

- Align in regular positions at first base, the pitcher's mound and behind the plate.
- Pitcher: start from the stretch, delivering the ball to home or attempt to pick off the man on first.
- First baseman: hold the runner at first or play behind the runner in a regular position to work on timing of the pick-off play.
- Runners: work on getting a good lead and concentrating on keys given by the pitchers.

**NOTE:** Work on the movement of the first baseman breaking toward the bag when the throw is made, prior to the drill. Specific pick-off plays should be worked on during this period to get the timing down.

# 148. Holding Runners Close—Second Base

**Primary Skill:** Defending runner on base

**Objective:** To practice and reinforce holding runners close to second base, as well as proper timing during pick-off plays.

**Equipment Needed:** Three baseballs, gloves, base and catcher's equipment

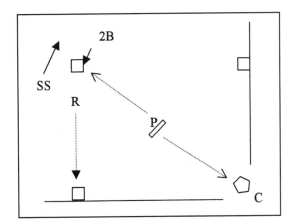

## COACH

- Talk through the drill prior to the start. Place the pitcher, the second baseman, the shortstop and the catcher in regular positions. Either have the second baseman hold the runner on or play behind the runner in a regular alignment.
- Use extra infielders as runners; indicate to the runners that this is a live offensive drill as well. Use another coach to monitor the runners.
- Remind the pitchers of pick-off techniques, options to keep the runners close and to throw off the runner's timing.
- Rotate other players after three or four repetitions.
- Monitor the infield's position before the pick-off attempt and after the throw to bag.

## PLAYER

- Align in regular positions at second base, shortstop, the pitcher's mound and behind the plate.
- Pitcher: start from the stretch, delivering the ball to home or attempt to pick off the man on first.
- The second baseman and the shortstop play in regular positions to work on the timing of the pick off plays as well as regular movement to keep the runner close.
- Runners: work on getting a good lead and concentrating on keys given by the pitchers.

**NOTE:** Work on the movement of the second baseman and the shortstop breaking toward the bag when throws are made, prior to the drill. Specific pick off plays should be worked on during this period to get the timing down.

# 149. Holding Runners Close—Third Base

**Primary Skill:** Defending runner on base

**Objective:** To practice and reinforce holding runners close to third base, as well as proper timing during pick-off plays.

**Equipment Needed:** Three baseballs, gloves, base and catcher's equipment

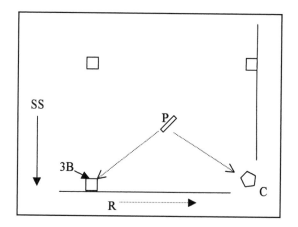

## COACH

- Talk through the drill prior to the start. Place pitcher, third baseman, shortstop and catcher in regular positions. Either have the third baseman hold the runner or play behind the runner in a regular alignment.
- Use extra infielders as runners; indicate to the runners that this is a live offensive drill as well. Use another coach to monitor the runners.
- Remind the pitchers of pick off techniques, options to keep the runners close and to throw off the runner's timing.
- Rotate other players after three or four repetitions.
- Monitor the infield's position before the pick off attempt and after the throw to the bag.

## PLAYER

- Align in regular positions at third base, shortstop, pitcher's mound and behind the plate.
- Pitcher: start from the stretch, delivering the ball to home or attempt to pick off the man on first.
- The third baseman and the shortstop play in regular positions to work on the timing of the pick off plays and back-up positioning as well as regular movement to keep the runner close.
- Runners: work on getting a good lead and concentrating on keys given by the pitchers.

**NOTE:** Work on movement of the third baseman and the shortstop breaking to the bag when throws are made, prior to the drill. Specific pick off plays should be worked on during this period to get the timing down.

# 150. Three-Ring Circus

**Primary Skill:** Defense

**Objective:** To involve three separate infield drills within the infield.

**Equipment Needed:** A bag of baseballs, gloves, bases, catcher's gear and a fungo bat

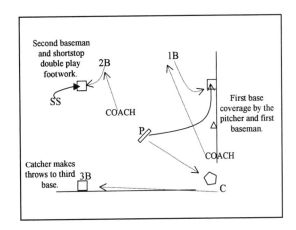

## COACH

- Set up the drill by putting the infielders in normal alignment.

- Explain each segment; these are drills that have already been developed separately from the three-ring circus.

- All three segments can start on the pitcher's motion (the middle infield drill can be run separately).

- One coach can monitor all three segments, but two or three coaches would be optimal for this situation.

## PLAYER

- Infielders align in normal positions.

- The pitcher will start the drill by making a live pitch to the catcher; this gives the catcher more realistic timing for the throw to third base and the pitcher moving to first.

**NOTE:** Adaptations can be made by plugging in other drills within the same framework.

# 151. Bunt Coverage

**Primary Skill:** Defense

**Objective:** To practice and fine-tune bunt coverage movements, as well as fielding techniques during those movements.

**Equipment Needed:** A bag of baseballs, gloves and bases

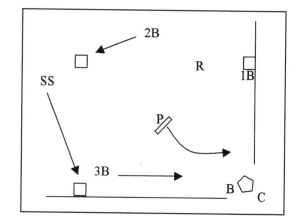

## COACH

- Decide before coming onto the field which bunt rotations are to be used.

- Set up the drill with the infielders in the proper alignment according to bunt situation. Talk and walk through rotations before running the live drill.

- Use extra infielders as runners; indicate to runners that this is a live offensive drill as well. Use another coach to monitor base runners.

- The pitcher starts the drill from the windup or the stretch to involve the batter incorporating live bunting repetitions.

- Monitor the infielders' position prior to the bunt and rotate the players after a few repetitions.

## PLAYER

- Align at infield positions according to bunt situations.

- Communicate with other infielders, so there is no confusion.

- The pitcher starts the drill from the windup or the stretch, depending on the situation. The ball can be delivered home or to first to hold the runners close.

- Perform the drill and rotate with other players.

**NOTE:** This drill is a framework for coaches to use their own techniques/plays during a bunt situation. A talk and walk through while teaching plays is optimal. If these plays are going to be used throughout the season, continue to review them.

# 152. Cut-Offs

**Primary Skills:** Defense

**Objective:** To practice and reinforce not only the proper throwing technique by outfielders, but also the proper cut-off positioning, bag coverage and communication by infielders.

**Equipment Needed:** A bag of baseballs, a fungo bat, gloves and bases

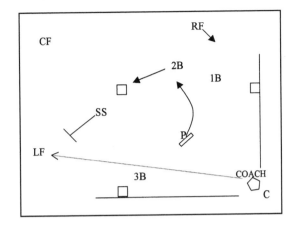

## COACH

- Set up the drill by initially using one base, either second base or third base. Have the outfielders form a single line and take repetitions. Use the infielders for cut-offs and to cover the bases.

- To start the drill, hit the ball to the outfielders and monitor techniques during the repetitions.

- One repetition can be taken or preferably two or three repetitions per rotation. This allows the players a better opportunity to correct mistakes immediately.

## PLAYER

- Form a single line in the outfield, step out in front to take repetitions. One infielder becomes cut-off, while another covers the bag.

- Communicate with the cut-off for throws to the bag, paying attention to the alignment of the cut-off with the bag and the outfielder.

- Take repetitions specified by the coach, then rotate to the back of the line.

**NOTE:** The cut-off technique, the bag coverage and the proper fielding/throwing should be taught prior to the drill.

# 153. Extra Base Cut-Offs

**Primary Skills:** Defense

**Objective:** To practice and reinforce not only the proper throwing technique by outfielders, but also the proper extra base cut-off positioning, bag coverage and communication by the infielders.

**Equipment Needed:** A bag of baseballs, a fungo bat, gloves and bases

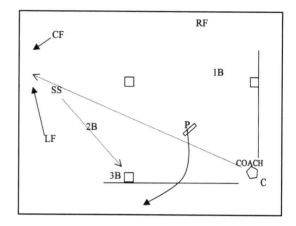

## COACH

- Set up the drill by initially using one base, either second base or third base. Have the outfielders form a single line to take repetitions. Use the infielders for cut-offs and to cover the bases.

- To start the drill, hit a ball over the head of the outfielders or in the gap, creating an extra base situation.

- One repetition can be taken or preferably two or three repetitions per rotation. This allows the players a better opportunity to correct mistakes immediately.

## PLAYER

- Form a single line in the outfield, step out in front to take repetitions.

- As an infielder, take cut-offs or become the trailing cut-off, while another covers the bag.

- When the ball is fielded make sure to make a good solid throw to the first cut-off man, in turn the next throw must be as good. The key is to not panic.

- Communicate with the cut-off for throws to the bag, paying attention to the alignment of the cut-off with the bag and the outfielder.

- Take repetitions specified by the coach, then rotate to the back of the line.

# 154. Cut-Offs with Runners

**Primary Skills:** Defense

**Objective:** To practice and reinforce not only the proper throwing technique by the outfielders, but also the proper cut-off positioning, bag coverage and communication by infielders with runners on base.

**Equipment Needed:** A bag of baseballs, a fungo bat, gloves and bases

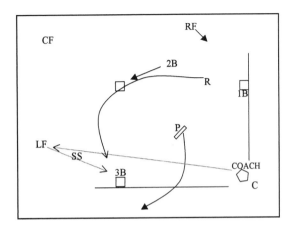

## COACH

• Set up the drill by initially using one base, either second base or third base. Have the outfielders form a single line to take repetitions. Use the infielders for cut-offs and to cover bases. Place the runners on either first base or second base attempting to take two bases.

• To start the drill, hit the ball to the outfielders; the runners will move when the ball is hit, attempting to take two bases.

• One repetition can be taken or preferably two or three repetitions per rotation. This allows the players a better opportunity to correct mistakes immediately.

## PLAYER

• Form a single line in the outfield; step out in front to take repetitions. One infielder becomes cut-off, while another covers the bag. The runners will start at either first base or third base attempting to move two bases.

• Communicate with the cut-off for throws to the bag, paying attention to the alignment of the cut-off with the bag and the outfielder. When making the throw, use enough velocity so the ball will make it to the base if it is not cut off.

• Take repetitions specified by the coach, then rotate to the back of the line.

# 155. Cut-Offs with Runner Tagging

**Primary Skills:** Defense

**Objective:** To practice and reinforce not only the proper throwing technique by outfielders, but also the proper cut-off positioning, bag coverage and communication by infielders with runners tagging up on base.

**Equipment Needed:** A bag of baseballs, a fungo bat, gloves and bases

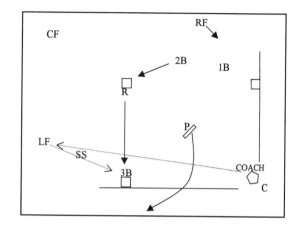

## COACH

- Set up the drill by initially using one base, either second base or third base. Have the outfielders form a single line to take repetitions. Use the infielders for the cut-offs and to cover bases. Place the runners on either first base, second base or third base.

- To start the drill, hit the ball to outfielders; the runners will tag when the ball is caught, attempting to take the next base.

- One repetition can be taken or preferably two or three repetitions per rotation. This allows the players a better opportunity to correct mistakes immediately.

## PLAYER

- Form a single line in the outfield; step out in front to take repetitions. One infielder becomes the cut-off, while another covers the bag. The runners will start at either first, second or third base and attempt to move to the next base on the catch.

- Communicate with the cut-off for throws to the bag, paying attention to alignment of cut-off with the bag and the outfielder. When making the throw, use enough velocity so the ball will make it to the base if it is not cut off.

- Take repetitions specified by the coach, then rotate to the back of the line.

# 156. Throws to Second Base—Third Baseman

**Primary Skill:** Throwing to a base

**Objective:** To practice and reinforce having the third baseman throw the ball to second base for a force play or the start of a double play.

**Equipment Needed:** Six baseballs, gloves, a fungo bat and a base

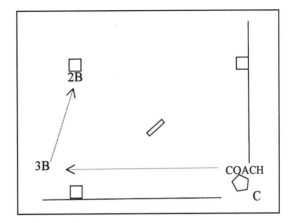

## COACH

- Demonstrate the proper technique prior to the start of the drill.

- Place the third baseman in a normal position and the second baseman a few feet off the second base bag to take throws from the third baseman.

- Stand at home plate to hit ground balls to the third baseman. After fielding the ground balls, the third baseman will use good mechanics when throwing the ball to the second baseman covering second base. The second baseman will work on double play footwork without throwing the ball to first base.

- Monitor the mechanics of the second and third baseman during the drill and rotate players every repetition.

## PLAYER

- Align at third base in normal positioning and at second base a few feet off the bag to take throws from the third baseman.

- Get in a good ready position at second and third base waiting for the coach to hit a ground ball to the third baseman. After the ball is fielded at third, make a good throw using the proper mechanics to second base.

- When the ball is received at second base, double play footwork is practiced without throwing the ball to first base.

- Take one repetition, then rotate with other players at the same position.

# 157. Throws to Second Base—First Baseman

**Primary Skill:** Throwing to second base

**Objective:** To practice and reinforce having the first baseman throw the ball to second base for a force play or the start of a double play.

**Equipment Needed:** Six baseballs, gloves, a fungo bat and a base

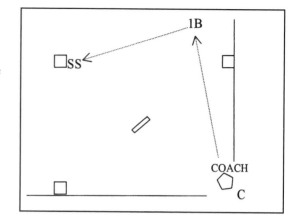

## COACH

- Demonstrate the proper technique prior to the start of the drill.

- Place the first baseman in a normal position and the shortstop a few feet off the second base bag to take throws from the first baseman.

- Stand at home plate and hit ground balls to the first baseman. After fielding the ground balls, the first baseman will use good mechanics when throwing the ball to the shortstop covering second base. The shortstop will work on double play footwork without throwing the ball to first base.

- Monitor the mechanics of the shortstop and the first baseman during the drill and rotate players every repetition.

## PLAYER

- Align at first base—holding the runner on the bag—and at shortstop a few feet off the bag to take throws from the first baseman.

- Get in a good ready position at shortstop and first base waiting for the coach to hit a ground ball to the first baseman. As the coach is hitting the ball, move off first base to a fielding position. After the ball is fielded at first, make a good throw using the proper mechanics to the shortstop covering the second base bag.

- When the ball is received at second base, double play footwork is practiced without throwing the ball to first base.

- Take one repetition, then rotate with other players at the same position.

# 158. Throws to Second Base—The Pitcher

**Primary Skill:** Throwing to second base

**Objective:** To practice and reinforce having the pitcher throw the ball to second base for a force play or the start of a double play.

**Equipment Needed:** Six baseballs, gloves, a fungo bat and a base

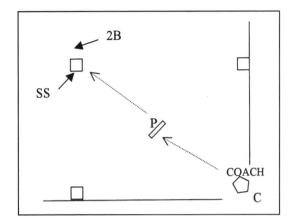

## COACH

- Demonstrate the proper technique prior to the start of the drill.
- Place pitcher in a normal position, the second baseman and shortstop a few feet off the second base bag to take throws from the pitcher.
- Stand at home plate and hit ground balls to the pitcher. After fielding the ground balls the pitcher will use good mechanics when throwing the ball to the shortstop or the second baseman covering second base. The shortstop and the second baseman will work on communication, as well as double play footwork without throwing the ball to first base.
- Monitor the mechanics of the second baseman, the shortstop and the pitcher during the drill and rotate players every repetition.

## PLAYER

- Align at the pitcher's mound as well as at shortstop and second base a few feet off the bag to take throws from the pitcher.
- Get in a good ready position at shortstop, second base and the mound waiting for the coach to hit a ground ball to the pitcher. After the ball is fielded on the mound, make a good throw using the proper mechanics to the shortstop or second baseman covering the second base bag.
- Before the ball is thrown to second, communicate with the other infielder. After the ball is received at second base, double play footwork is practiced without throwing the ball to first base.
- Take one repetition, then rotate with other players at the same position.

# 159. Infield/Outfield—Outfield Segment

**Primary Skill:** Defense

**Objective:** To practice and reinforce not only the proper throwing technique by outfielders, but also the proper cut-off positioning, bag coverage and communication by infielders.

**Equipment Needed:** Six baseballs, a fungo bat, gloves and bases

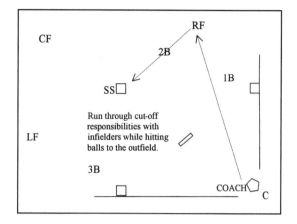

## COACH

• Set up the drill by aligning the infield and the outfield in normal positions.
• Dictate where the ball is to be thrown and keep the drill moving and upbeat.
• When hitting to the outfield, stand at the pitcher's mound—this helps to control the ball. Give each outfielder two or three repetitions to keep their arms loose.
• Have players throw to second base and then to third base before moving to the next outfield position.
• Hit the balls to the outfield with a purpose: fly balls, ground balls and balls in the gaps.
• As soon as ball is being thrown to the base, another ball should be hit.

## PLAYER

• Outfielders:
  —Be in a good ready position and listen for the coach's directions.
  —Field the ball and throw through the cut-off man's head.
  —Use the proper techniques in all situations: fly balls, ground balls, balls in the gaps.
• Infielders:
  —Perform cut-off rotations.
  —Communicate between the bag coverage and the cut-off man.
  —The first baseman feeds the coach balls at the pitcher's mound.
  —The catcher remains at home plate.
  —After the ball is thrown to the bag, throw to third base, throw to home, then to the coach.
  —Make throws quickly, without wasting time—as soon as the ball is received get rid of it.

**NOTE:** After the outfielder makes the last throw to home plate, run off the field or to center field for fly balls during the infield segment. Also, the catcher makes a snap throw to third base after the last outfielder has made a throw on the last repetition to home plate.

# 160. Infield/Outfield—Infield Segment

**Primary Skill:** Defense

**Objective:** To practice the proper fielding technique and throws to bases by infielders.

**Equipment Needed:** Six baseballs, a fungo bat, gloves and bases

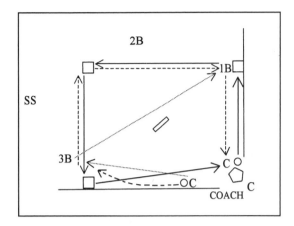

## COACH

· · · · · · · · · · · · · · · · · · · · · · · · ·

- Start the infielders on the edge of the grass.

- Set the tempo by hitting balls quickly; don't wait until the ball returns to the catcher before hitting the next repetition.

- Sequence of repetitions:

  —The infielders are on the edge of the infield grass fielding ground balls and making throws to the catcher.

  —Throw the ball out in front of home plate for the catcher to throw to first base, then the throw goes around the horn; first base to second base to third base, then to home.

  —Throw the ball out in front of home plate for the catcher to throw to third base, third baseman to throw to second base, second baseman to throw to first base, first baseman to throw home.

  —The infielders are in normal positions fielding ground balls, then making throws to first base by each infield position.

  —The infielders are in normal positions fielding ground balls, then making throws to second base for double plays.

  —Hit infield fly balls to the infielders in normal positions; this is optional.

  —The infielders are on the edge of the infield grass fielding ground balls and throwing home, then following the throw home for a rolled ball that is thrown to first base.

*(continued)*

# 160. Infield/Outfield—Infield Segment *(continued)*

## PLAYER

- Listen for the coach's instruction and use the proper technique throughout the drill.

- First align on edge off the grass for throws to home, keeping the ball in front of you, knocking it down, then making a quick throw home.

- Move to normal alignments for making throws to first base and throwing the ball around the horn after the catcher makes throw to first and third base.

- Next, field the balls to make the throw to second base for double plays.

- Finally, align again on the edge of the grass to take ground balls and make throws home. Follow throws home for another ball from the catcher, then make a throw to first base and run off the field.

# 161. Situations—Full Defense

**Primary Skill:** Defense and offense

**Objective:** To practice and reinforce situations that may occur during a game, such as cut-off movement, bunt coverage, first and third, pitcher covering first base, defensively as well as offensively.

**Equipment Needed:** Six baseballs, a fungo bat, gloves, catcher's gear and bases

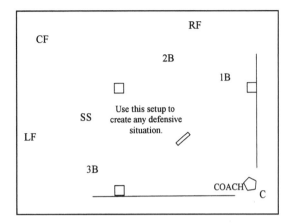

## COACH

• Set up the drill by aligning the infield and the outfield in normal positions.

• Use extra outfielders and infielders as the runners; indicate to the runners this is a live drill offensively as well. Use another coach responsible for the runners. This is a good time to practice signals.

• Present a situation, such as number of outs, runners on base, etc., to the players before ball is hit.

• Also create situations that need work, such as cut-off movements, bunts, first and third, steals, etc.

• Put the ball in play by hitting or bunting it somewhere on the playing field.

• Rotate other players in any manner, the number of outs, repetitions, etc.

## PLAYER

• Align in the normal fielding positions.

• Listen for situations and try to recognize possible plays before the coach's cue.

• Everything starts on the pitcher's motion. The ball is live simulating a game situation.

• The runner starts next to home plate on the first base side but does not move until the coach puts the ball in play. The ball is live—run as if in game situation.

• Take the number of repetitions specified by the coach before rotating.

# 162. Situations—Infield Only

**Primary Skill:** Defense

**Objective:** To practice and reinforce situations that may occur in the infield during a game, defensively as well as offensively.

**Equipment Needed:** Six baseballs, gloves, a fungo bat, catcher's gear and bases

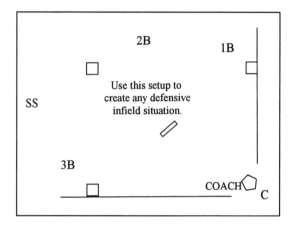

## COACH

- Set up the drill by aligning the infield in normal positions.
- Use the outfielders as the runners; indicate to the runners this is a live drill offensively as well. Use another coach to watch the runners.
- Present the situation, such as number of outs, runners on base, etc., to the players before ball is hit.
- Also create situations that need work, such as bunts, first and third, steals, etc. Play starts on the pitcher's windup or the stretch motion.
- Put the ball in play after the pitch by hitting or bunting it somewhere in the infield.
- Rotate other infielders in any manner, number of outs, reps, etc.

## PLAYER

- Align in normal fielding positions.
- Listen for situations and try to recognize possible plays before the coach's cue.
- Everything starts on the pitcher's motion. The ball is live simulating a game situation.
- The runner starts next to home plate on the first base side, but does not move until the coach puts the ball in play. The ball is live—run as if in a game situation.
- Take the number of repetitions specified by the coach before rotating.

**NOTE:** If the ball goes into the outfield, the runners should advance one base.

# 163.  Batting Practice—Field Setup I

**Primary Skill:** Hitting and defense

**Objective:** To make efficient use of players and field space while reinforcing fielding skills as well as batting skills.

**Equipment Needed:** Pitching screen, bag of baseballs, bats, home plate, batting cage or field

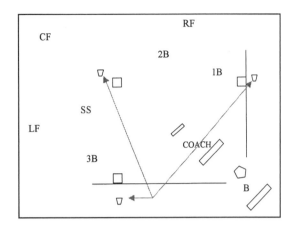

## COOACH

- Place empty buckets or other containers near first, second and third bases. The container with the balls will start with the batting practice pitcher.

- The balls hit to the infielders will be thrown to first base; the balls will then be placed in container at first base. The balls hit to the outfield will be thrown to second or third base. The coach will designate the base; the balls will be placed in containers at those bases.

- When the pitcher's container is empty, the containers from first, second and third bases are brought to the mound and emptied.

## PLAYER

- Align at regular positions with a partner, so when one is fielding the other protects by watching the batter.

- Play each ball as a live ball, throw to the designated bag, cover designated bag and move to cut-off positions.

- As soon as the pitcher's container is empty, run other containers to the mound and empty.

**NOTE:** This keeps batting practice moving and gives each fielder a purpose instead of standing and waiting for the next ball.

# 164. Batting Practice—Field Setup II

**Primary Skill:** Hitting and defense

**Objective:** To make efficient use of players and field space while reinforcing fielding skills as well as batting skills.

**Equipment Needed:** Pitching screen, bag of baseballs, bats, home plate, batting cage or field

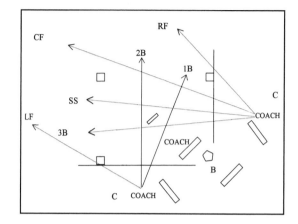

## COACH

- Set up a regular infield and outfield, but with two players at each position.

- Use two coaches or players to hit ground balls and fly balls. Also, use a player to catch throws from the infielders and the outfielders.

- The coach or player along the first base line will hit to the shortstop and the third base, as well as to right field and center. The coach or player along the third base line will hit to second base and first base, as well as to left field.

- If extra screens are available use them for protection on the home plate side of the coach or player hitting ground balls.

## PLAYER

- Align at the regular infield and outfield positions with a partner, so when one is fielding the other protects by watching the batter.

- Play the ball off the bat of the batting practice batter, while the other takes the ball from the coach or player hitting from the foul lines.

- Switch on every three repetitions.

**NOTE:** This keeps batting practice moving and gives each fielder a purpose instead of standing and waiting for the next ball. The coach or player hitting ground balls should alternate balls between pitches, so an infielder or outfielder doesn't have two balls at the same time.

# 165. Live Sacrifice Bunt

**Primary Skill:** Bunting

**Objective:** To practice and reinforce the proper bunt technique versus live pitching.

**Equipment Needed:** A bag of baseballs, batting helmet, home plate, bats, two cones or two buckets

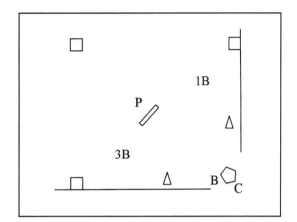

## COACH

- Set up the drill on the diamond or in gym with two fielders, a pitcher, a catcher and a batter. Place two containers, one along the third base line and the other along the first base line, both approximately 10 to 15 feet away from home plate.

- The pitcher is throwing live pitches to the catcher. This time also can be used to work on pitches as well. Two other players help field the balls and then rotate into the batter's position.

- Initially, emphasize batter preparation before the pitcher releases the ball and then work on technique and contact with the ball. Finally, progress to the balls being bunted down the first and third base lines, targeting containers.

## PLAYER

- Align as a batter while another pitches and two others field the bunts.

- Focus on the timing of the preparation, the proper bunting technique and making contact with the ball.

- Bunt the ball down either the third base line or the first base line, aiming for the containers.

- Rotate after five repetitions.

# 166. Live Bunting for Base Hit

**Primary Skill:** Bunting

**Objective:** To practice and reinforce the proper bunt technique versus live pitching.

**Equipment Needed:** A bag of baseballs, batting helmet, home plate, bats, two cones or two buckets

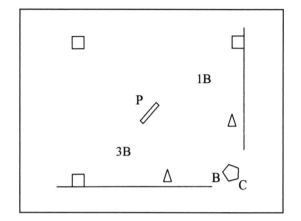

## COACH

- Set up the drill on the diamond or in gym with two fielders, a pitcher, a catcher and a batter. Place two containers, one along the third base line and the other along the first base line, both approximately 10 to 15 feet away from home plate.

- The pitcher is throwing live pitches to the catcher. This time can also be used to work on pitches as well. Two other players help field the balls and then rotate into the batter's position.

- Initially, emphasize mechanics of the bunt as well as being patient and then contact with the ball. Finally, progress to the balls being bunted down the first and third base lines, targeting containers.

## PLAYER

- Align as a batter while another pitches and two others field the bunts.

- Focus on the mechanics of the bunt, being patient and making contact with the ball.

- Bunt the ball down either the third base line or the first base line, aiming for the containers.

- Rotate after five repetitions.

# 167. Live Combo Bunt Drill

**Primary Skill:** Bunting

**Objective:** To practice and reinforce the proper bunt technique versus live pitching.

**Equipment Needed:** A bag of baseballs, batting helmet, home plate, bats, two cones or two buckets

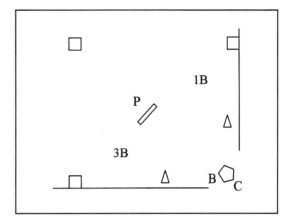

## COACH

- Set up the drill on the diamond or in the gym with two fielders, a pitcher, a catcher and a batter. Place two containers, one along the third base line and the other along the first base line, both approximately 10 to 15 feet away from home plate.

- The pitcher is throwing live pitches to the catcher. This time can be used to work on pitches as well. Two other players help field the balls, then rotate into the batter's position.

- Initially, emphasize batter preparation before the pitcher releases the ball and then work on technique and contact with the ball. Finally, progress to the balls being bunted down the first and third base lines, targeting containers.

- Have the batter alternate bunts from a sacrifice to a bunt for a base hit, about three to five repetitions for each bunt.

## PLAYER

- Align as a batter while another pitches and two others field the bunts.

- Focus on the timing of the preparation, the proper bunting technique and making contact with ball.

- Alternate bunts from a sacrifice to a bunt for a base hit. Bunt the ball down either the third base line or the first base line, aiming for the containers.

- Rotate after three to five repetitions for each bunt.

# 168. Pride Drill

**Primary Skill:** Conditioning, team pride

**Objective:** To develop team pride and conditioning by running on and off the field.

**Equipment Needed:** None

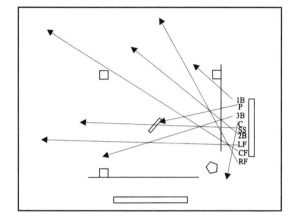

## COACH

- Explain the purpose and expectations of the drill prior to beginning.

- Split the team into two or three groups depending on the total number of players. Initially have the players assigned to regular positions.

- Start each group on the bench and then cue the players to hustle to positions on the field. Once the players are set, hit a ball to be played. After the ball is played, the players will then hustle off the field to the bench.

- When the first group of players is on the bench, have the second group run onto the field and repeat the drill with the second group.

- Have each group take five repetitions and monitor each repetition closely.

## PLAYER

- Split into groups and positions designated by the coach. Sit on the bench until the coach gives a cue to run to designated positions.

- Once the cue is given, hustle to positions on the field. When the coach hits a ball, make a play then hustle off the field to the bench.

- Repeat repetitions five times.

# 169. Pepper Drill

**Primary Skill:** Quickness and agility

**Objective:** To reinforce hand/eye coordination as well as quickness and agility.

**Equipment Needed:** A baseball, a bat and gloves

```
  P  P  P  P            P  P  P  P
P           P        P           P
    B                    B

  P  P  P  P            P  P  P  P
P           P        P           P
    B                    B
```

## COACH

- Demonstrate the drill prior to beginning, then put players in groups of four or five.

- Have one player position as the batter about 15 feet from the other players in the group. The remaining players position in a semicircle in front of the batter.

- Each batter takes five or six repetitions before switching with other players in the group. Monitor each group closely.

## PLAYER

- Get into groups of four or five with a batter aligning 15 feet from the fielders in the group. As a fielder, align in a semicircle in front of the batter.

- As a batter, choke up on the bat, taking only small short chops at the ball and remembering the fielders are in close proximity.

- One fielder will throw the ball to the batter; when the ball is hit, the fielder receiving the ball will then throw it to the batter.

- Repeat this procedure five or six times before batter rotates with the fielders.

# 170. Pregame Drill

**Primary Skill:** Defense

**Objective:** To reinforce defensive situations prior to the start of the game.

**Equipment Needed:** Six baseballs, gloves, a fungo bat and catcher's gear

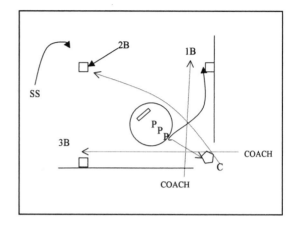

## COACH

- Explain the drill prior to the first time through the drill.
- Place the catchers behind home plate in full gear, the pitchers on the front half of the mound and the infielders in normal positions.
- Have the pitchers pitch the ball to the catcher half speed, then hit a ground ball to the first baseman. The pitcher will then cover first base receiving a toss from the first baseman. The catcher will make a throw to the second base bag to the second baseman or the shortstop. The second baseman and the shortstop should also work on the cut-off play during a first and third situation.
- Stand on the third base side of home plate to hit ground balls to the first baseman.
- Another coach or player, standing on the first base side of home plate, will hit ground balls to the third baseman.
- Work through each segment of the drill so that each player gets three to five repetitions.

## PLAYER

- Catchers: Align behind home plate in full gear, receiving pitches from the pitcher. After receiving pitches, make a throw to the second base bag.
- Pitchers: Align on the front half of the mound. Perform the windup making a pitch to the catcher, then cover first base after the coach hits a ground ball to the first baseman.
- First baseman: Align in normal infield position ready to take ground balls from the coach or player standing on the third base side of home plate. After receiving the ground ball, make a toss to the pitcher covering the first base bag.
- Second baseman and shortstop: Align in a position close to the second base bag to take throws from the catcher. While one is receiving the throw, the other backs up. Also work on cut-offs for the first and third situation.
- Third baseman: Align in normal infield position ready to take ground balls from the coach or player standing on the first base side of home plate.

# 171. All Purpose Drill

**Primary Skill:** Defense

**Objective:** To reinforce defensive situations that might arise during the game.

**Equipment Needed:** A bag of baseballs, bats, tees, gloves and catcher's gear

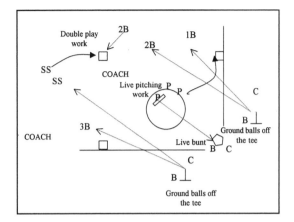

## COACH

- Explain the drill prior to the first time through.
- Place the catchers behind home plate in full gear, the pitchers on the first base side of the mound with one pitcher standing on the rubber and at least two infielders at each position. Also, place two batters with tees along the first base line and the third base line, while another batter stands at home plate.
- Use at least one other coach to help monitor the drills.
- Work through each segment of the drill so that each player gets three to five repetitions.

## PLAYER

- Catchers: Align behind home plate in full gear; receive live pitches from the pitcher on the mound.
- Pitchers: One aligns on the rubber to throw 25 pitches to the catcher, while the others align to the left of the mound. If aligned to the left, break for first base to cover on ground balls hit off the tee along the first base line. Switch after each repetition.
- First baseman: Align in a normal infield position ready to take ground balls off the tee along the first base line. After receiving the ground ball, make a toss to the pitcher covering the first base bag.
- Second baseman: Align in a position close to the second base bag to take throws from the shortstop and third baseman. While one is receiving the throw, the other takes ground balls and throws to first base.
- Shortstop: Align in a normal position taking ground balls off the tee along the third baseline, then make throws to second base.

*(continued)*

# 171. All Purpose Drill *(continued)*

- Third baseman: Align in a normal infield position ready to take ground balls off the tee along the third base line, then make throws to second base.
- Batters: When hitting off the tee use good mechanics to hit ground balls to the infielders. Also, take a partner to catch the balls coming back from the first and second baseman. If aligned at home plate, practice live bunting off pitches being thrown by the pitcher.

**NOTE:** Extra players including the outfielders will become the hitters during this drill. Work in infielders, pitchers and catchers after hitting.

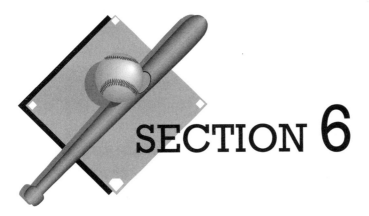

# SECTION **6**

# BATTING

*To prepare well is to succeed.*

—BENJAMIN FRANKLIN

# 172. Classroom Stance and Alignment Drill

**Primary Skill:** Stance and alignment.

**Objective:** To develop the proper stance and good alignment when in the batter's box.

**Equipment Needed:** Three or four home plates

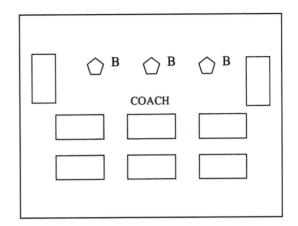

## COACH

- Demonstrate the proper stance and alignment before starting the drill.
- Clear a space by moving the desks to the side of the room. The space should be big enough for three or four batters to get into the stance and align at the plate.
- Then place three or four home plates 6 feet apart across the room.
- Put one player at each home plate, monitoring techniques closely. Rotate the players through the drill after observing each batter.

## PLAYER

- Align at one of the home plates first in the proper alignment and then the proper stance.
- Wait until the coach checks alignment and stance before rotating with other players.

# 173. Classroom Load Drill

**Primary Skill:** Swing preparation

**Objective:** To develop the load, keeping the hands and weight back to prepare the body for the swing.

**Equipment Needed:** Three or four home plates

## COACH

- Demonstrate the load and when to initiate it before starting the drill.

- Clear a space by moving the desks to the side of the room. The space should be big enough for three or four batters to get into a stance and align at the plate.

- Then place three or four home plates 6 feet apart across the room. Give the batters a pitching motion for timing to initiate the load.

- Put one player at each home plate, monitoring the techniques closely. Rotate the players through the drill after observing each batter.

## PLAYER

- Align at one of the home plates, first in the proper alignment and then the proper stance.

- Watch the pitchers motion to initiate the load. Take five repetitions before rotating with other players.

# 174. Classroom Swing Drill

**Primary Skill:** Swing mechanics

**Objective:** To develop and practice the proper swing mechanics.

**Equipment Needed:** Three or four home plates

B    B    B

COACH

## COACH

- Demonstrate the proper swing mechanics before starting the drill.
- Clear a space by moving the desks to the side of the room. The space should be big enough for three or four batters to get into a stance and align at the plate.
- Then place three or four home plates 6 feet apart across the room.
- Put one player at each home plate, monitoring the techniques closely. Rotate the players through the drill after each batter has taken 10 good swings.

## PLAYER

- Align at one of the home plates first in the proper alignment and then the proper stance.
- Perform the swing starting with the load to completion of the swing; emphasize throwing the hands through the strike zone.
- Take 10 swings before rotating with other players.

# 175. Classroom One-Arm Swing Drill—Front Hand

**Primary Skill:** Swing mechanics

**Objective:** To develop and practice the proper mechanics of the swing using only the front hand.

**Equipment Needed:** Three or four home plates

## COACH

- Demonstrate the proper swing mechanics with the front hand before starting the drill.

- Clear a space by moving the desks to the side of the room. The space should be big enough for three or four batters to get into a stance and align at the plate.

- Then place three or four home plates 6 feet apart across the room.

- Put one player at each home plate, monitoring the techniques closely. Rotate the players through the drill after each batter has taken 10 good swings.

## PLAYER

- Align at one of the home plates first in the proper alignment and then the proper stance.

- Perform the swing with the front hand only starting with the load to the completion of the swing; emphasize throwing the front hand through the strike zone. Place the back hand behind the back while swinging with the front hand.

- Take 10 swings before rotating with other players.

# 176. Classroom One-Arm Swing Drill—Back Hand

**Primary Skill:** Swing mechanics

**Objective:** To develop and practice
the proper mechanics of the swing
using only the back hand.

**Equipment Needed:** Three or four
home plates

B B B

COACH

## COACH

- Demonstrate the proper swing mechanics with the back hand before starting the drill.
- Clear a space by moving the desks to the side of the room. The space should be big enough for three or four batters to get into a stance and align at the plate.
- Then place three or four home plates 6 feet apart across the room.
- Put one player at each home plate, monitoring the techniques closely. Rotate the players through the drill after each batter has taken 10 good swings.

## PLAYER

- Align at one of the home plates first in the proper alignment and then the proper stance.
- Perform the swing with the back hand starting with the load to the completion of the swing; emphasize throwing the back hand through the strike zone. Place the front hand behind the back while swinging with the back hand.
- Take 10 swings before rotating with other players.

# 177. Isometric Swing Drill

**Primary Skill:** Conditioning

**Objective:** To strengthen the muscles involved in the swing.

**Equipment Needed:** Bat

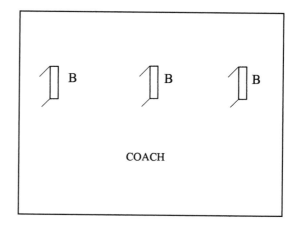

## COACH

- Demonstrate the proper technique prior to the beginning of the drill.
- Place the hitters with a bat at a stationary object such as a pole, a fence or the backstop. Start the hitters in the contact position against the pole. Let them push and try to complete the swing and hold the position for 10 seconds.
- Monitor each hitter for the proper mechanics. Have each hitter perform the drill for 5 to 10 repetitions.

## PLAYER

- Start the drill with a bat standing next to a stationary object such as a pole, a fence or the backstop.
- Place the bat against the object to simulate the contact position. Push against the object with force, trying to complete the swing. Hold this position for 10 seconds, repeating 5 to 10 times.

# 178. Weighted Bat Drill

**Primary Skill:** Conditioning

**Objective:** To strengthen the muscles involved in the swing.

**Equipment Needed:** Weighted bat

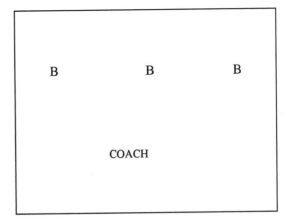

## COACH

- Explain the purpose of the drill before beginning.
- Make sure each player has a bat that can be controlled; if it's too heavy, bad habits can develop.
- Each player takes 50 swings. Monitor the swings closely, making sure the proper mechanics are being used.
- This is a good off-season drill.

## PLAYER

- Pick a heavier bat, but one that can be controlled through the swing.
- Perform good swings with the proper mechanics through the swing. Take approximately 50 swings a day.

# 179. Strike Zone Drill

**Primary Skill:** Strike zone recognition

**Objective:** To develop the recognition of pitches in the strike zone.

**Equipment Needed:** Bat and batter's helmet

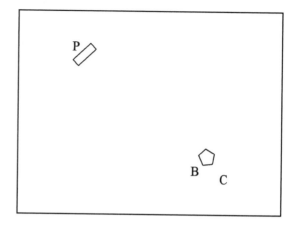

## COACH

- Explain the purpose of the drill before beginning.

- Have the batter stand in the batter's box during bullpen work by the pitcher or pregame warm-up. Make sure the batter has a helmet for protection.

- Emphasize to the batter the importance of the proper mechanics on each pitch. Even though the batter is not swinging, the proper focus on each pitch is essential to recognize pitches in the strike zone.

- Monitor the batter's repetitions, closely watching for the proper mechanics.

## PLAYER

- Stand in the batter's box with a helmet and a bat for the purpose of watching pitches to practice recognizing balls in the strike zone.

- Do not swing at any pitches, but use the proper mechanics on each one to prepare to hit pitches in the strike zone.

- Stand in the batter's box for approximately 25 pitches.

# 180. Load Drill

**Primary Skill:** Timing

**Objective:** To practice the load, keeping the hands and weight back to prepare the body for the swing.

**Equipment Needed:** Bat and batter's helmet

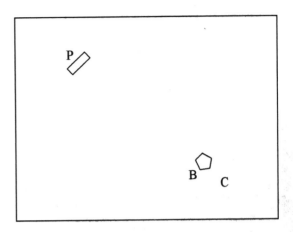

## COACH

- Explain the purpose of the drill before beginning.

- Have the batter stand in the batter's box during a bullpen workout of the pitcher or during a pregame warm-up. Make sure the batter has a helmet for protection.

- Emphasize to the batter the importance of loading on each pitch. Even though the batter is not swinging, the proper loading on each pitch is essential.

- Monitor the batter's repetitions, closely watching for the proper mechanics.

## PLAYER

- Stand in the batter's box with a helmet and a bat for the purpose of loading on each pitch to practice proper timing and weight distribution.

- Do not swing at any pitches, but use the proper loading on each one to prepare to hit pitches in the strike zone. Hands and weight should be back after the load takes place.

- Stand in the batter's box for approximately 25 pitches.

# 181. Mirror Drill

**Primary Skill:** Swing mechanics

**Objective:** To analyze the proper mechanics of the batter's swing.

**Equipment Needed:** Bat and a mirror

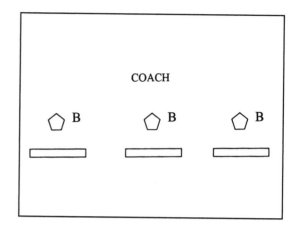

## COACH

- Explain the purpose of the drill before beginning.
- Place the batters with a bat in front of the mirror, performing the proper swing mechanics.
- Help each batter analyze the swing by asking guided questions so the batter is making corrections.

## PLAYER

- Stand in front of a mirror with a bat, performing the proper mechanics of the swing.
- Check the mirror to see if the mechanics are being performed properly. Check with the coach to correct problem areas.

# 182. Hip Drill

**Primary Skill:** Hip rotation

**Objective:** To develop and reinforce proper hip rotation during the swing.

**Equipment Needed:** Bat

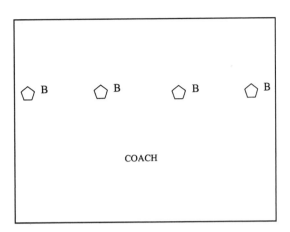

## COACH

- Explain and demonstrate the proper technique before beginning.
- Have each player start with a bat, placing it behind the back resting on the forearms.
- From this position the batter takes a stride rotating the hips open.
- Monitor each batter closely, helping to create the proper mechanics. The batters should perform this drill 10 times.

## PLAYER

- Start in a normal batter's box stance and then place the bat behind your back so it is resting on the forearms.
- From this position, take a normal stride rotating the hips open when completing a swing.
- Repeat technique approximately 10 times.

# 183. Towel Drill

**Primary Skill:** Swing mechanics

**Objective:** To develop and reinforce hand quickness during the swing to the point of contact with the ball.

**Equipment Needed:** Four towels and a home plate

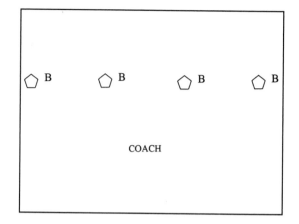

## COACH

- Explain and demonstrate the proper mechanics before beginning the drill.
- Set up four home plates 8 to 10 feet apart with a towel at each home plate.
- Place a batter at each plate with the towel in hand. Start each player in a good stance and alignment with the towel draped over the back shoulder holding the end of the towel with both hands as if gripping a bat.
- From this position the batter will then perform the swing, snapping hands through the strike zone. Hand quickness is essential in order to swing the towel through the zone.
- Monitor batters' swings closely, making corrections and providing encouragement when necessary.

## PLAYER

- Set up at one of the home plates in a good stance and alignment with a towel draped over your back shoulder. Grab the end of the towel with both hands as if gripping the bat.
- From this position perform a swing starting with load first and then snap your hands through the strike zone. Hand quickness is essential to get the towel moving through the strike zone.
- Take 10 swings before rotating with other players.

# 184.  Rolled-Up Towel Drill

**Primary Skill:** Swing mechanics

**Objective:** To reinforce the back arm position prior to and during the swing.

**Equipment Needed:** Rolled-up towel, home plate, bat and four baseballs

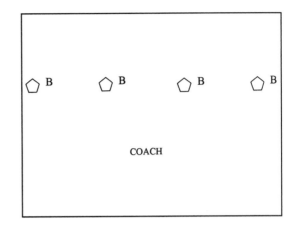

## COACH

- Explain the purpose and demonstrate the mechanics of the drill before beginning.
- Use this drill as a prescription to correct a looping swing and in conjunction with the "Tee Drills" or the "Flip-Toss Drill."
- Place batter in a good stance and the proper alignment at home plate. Tuck the rolled-up towel under the back arm while the batter is in a good stance.
- The towel will remain under the arm until the swing forces the back arm to extend.
- Monitor the batter's swing; emphasize to the batter not to hold the towel tightly.

## PLAYER

- Align at home plate in a good stance and the proper alignment. Tuck the rolled-up towel under the back arm, holding it lightly against the ribs.
- Take swings off the tee: flip-toss or dry swings to reinforce keeping the back arm close to body prior to the swing. The towel will remain under the arm until the back arm extends through the swing.
- Take 10 swings before rotating with other players.

# 185. Single-Arm Towel Drill—Back Hand

**Primary Skill:** Swing mechanics

**Objective:** To develop and reinforce back hand quickness during the swing to the point of contact with the ball.

**Equipment Needed:** Four towels and a home plate

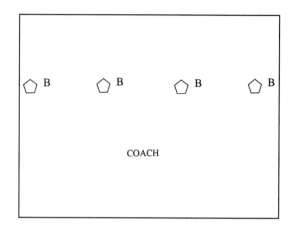

## COACH

- Explain and demonstrate the proper mechanics before beginning the drill.

- Set up four home plates 8 to 10 feet apart with a towel at each home plate.

- Place a batter at each plate with a towel in hand. Start each player in a good stance and alignment with the towel draped over the back shoulder holding the end of the towel with the back hand as if gripping a bat, placing the front hand behind the back.

- From this position the batter will then perform the swing, snapping the hand through the strike zone. Hand quickness is essential in order to swing the towel through the zone.

- Monitor the batters' swings closely, making corrections and providing encouragement when necessary.

## PLAYER

- Set up at one of the home plates in a good stance and alignment with a towel draped over your back shoulder. Grab the end of the towel with your back hand as if gripping the bat, placing the front hand behind the back.

- From this position perform a swing starting with the load first and then snap the hand through the strike zone. Hand quickness is essential to get the towel moving through the strike zone.

- Take 10 swings before rotating with other players.

# 186. Single-Arm Towel Drill—Front Hand

**Primary Skill:** Swing mechanics

**Objective:** To develop and reinforce front hand quickness during the swing to the point of contact with the ball.

**Equipment Needed:** Four towels and a home plate

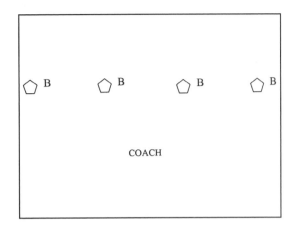

## COACH

- Explain and demonstrate the proper mechanics before beginning the drill.

- Set up four home plates 8 to 10 feet apart with a towel at each home plate.

- Place a batter at each plate with a towel in hand. Start each player in a good stance and alignment with the towel draped over the back shoulder holding the end of the towel with the front hand as if gripping a bat, placing the back hand behind the back.

- From this position the batter will then perform the swing, snapping the hand through the strike zone. Hand quickness is essential in order to swing the towel through the zone.

- Monitor the batters' swings closely, making corrections and providing encouragement when necessary.

## PLAYER

- Set up at one of the home plates in a good stance and alignment with a towel draped over the back shoulder. Grab the end of the towel with the front hand as if gripping a bat, placing the back hand behind the back. From this position perform a swing starting with the load first and then snap the hand through the strike zone. Hand quickness is essential to get the towel moving through the strike zone.

- Take 10 swings before rotating with other players.

# 187.  Throw Drill

**Primary Skill:** Swing mechanics

**Objective:** To reinforce the proper hand position and movement toward the ball during the swing.

**Equipment Needed:** Four baseballs, rag balls or tennis balls, a net or screen and a home plate

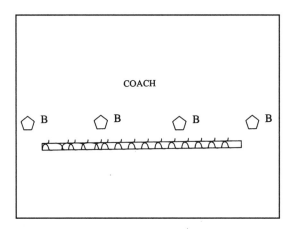

## COACH

- Explain and demonstrate the proper technique prior to beginning.
- Place the batter in a proper stance and proper positioning next to home plate with a ball in the back hand in front of a net or screen.
- Batters should take 10 throws before rotating with other batters.
- Monitor each batter's technique carefully, making corrections and providing encouragement when appropriate.

© 2001 by Prentice Hall

## PLAYER

- Start in a normal batter's box stance with a ball in the back hand, while the other hand holds onto the backhand wrist.
- From this position perform the load, the stride and the swing. On the swing the backhand will release the ball right at the contact point.
- Repeat this technique 10 times before switching with other batters.

**NOTE:** This is a good drill to practice hitting an inside and outside pitch as well.

# 188. Flip-Toss Drill

**Primary Skill:** Hitting

**Objective:** To practice and reinforce the proper hitting technique, which involves feet, hands, weight, stride and swing.

**Equipment Needed:** Four baseballs, home plate, bat and a screen or fence

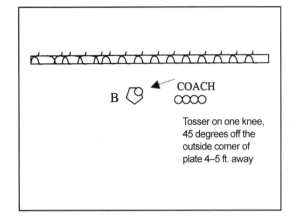

COACH

B

Tosser on one knee, 45 degrees off the outside corner of plate 4–5 ft. away

## COACH

• Demonstrate the proper tossing technique to the players—tosser should be on one knee, 45 degrees off the outside corner of the plate, 4 or 5 feet away. This technique is very important—if the toss is not performed properly, the hitting repetitions will suffer.

• After modeling the toss, allow the players to pair up, and monitor the hitter and the tosser.

## PLAYER

• Pair up: one is hitting while the other is tossing.

• Each pair should have approximately four balls, preferably tennis or rag balls for safety.

• Take 10 swings, paying close attention to the stance, hand position, stride and swing.

• Switch after 10 repetitions.

**NOTE:** Do not toss balls quickly; give the hitter a chance to reset. It is important for the hitter to develop good habits.

# 189.  Flip-Toss Drill—Hitting the Inside Pitch

**Primary Skill:** Inside pitch swing

**Objective:** To practice and reinforce the proper hitting mechanics for a pitch on the inside part of the plate.

**Equipment Needed:** Four baseballs, home plate, bat and a screen or fence

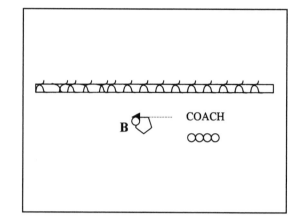

## COACH

- Demonstrate the proper tossing technique to the players. This technique is very important—if the toss is not performed properly the hitting repetitions will suffer. The tosser flips the balls to the front hip and knee of the batter to simulate inside pitches.

- After modeling the toss, allow the players to pair up, and monitor both the hitter and the tosser.

## PLAYER

- Pair up: one hits while the other tosses. The tosser flips the balls to the front hip and knee of the batter to simulate inside pitches.

- Each pair should have approximately four balls, preferably tennis or rag balls for safety.

- Take 10 swings, paying close attention to the stance, hand position, stride and swing.

- Switch after 10 repetitions.

**NOTE:** Do not toss the balls quickly; give the hitter a chance to reset. It is important for the hitter to develop good habits.

# 190. Flip-Toss Drill—Hitting the Outside Pitch

**Primary Skill:** Outside pitch swing

**Objective:** To practice and reinforce the proper hitting mechanics for a pitch on the outside part of the plate.

**Equipment Needed:** Four baseballs, home plate, bat and a screen or fence

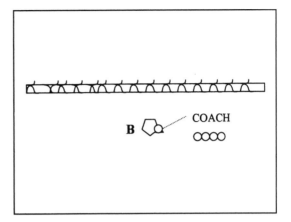

## COACH

- Demonstrate the proper tossing technique to the players. This technique is very important—if the toss is not performed properly, the hitting repetitions will suffer. The tosser flips the balls to the back hip and knee of the batter to simulate outside pitches.

- After modeling the toss, allow the players to pair up, and monitor both the hitter and the tosser.

## PLAYER

- Pair up: one is hitting while the other is tossing. The tosser flips the balls to the back hip and knee of the batter to simulate outside pitches.

- Each pair should have approximately four balls, preferably tennis or rag balls for safety.

- Take 10 swings, paying close attention to the stance, hand position, stride and swing.

- Switch after 10 repetitions.

**NOTE:** Do not toss balls quickly; give hitter a chance to reset. It is important for the hitter to develop good habits.

# 191. Flip-Toss Drill—Lead Hand Swing

**Primary Skill:** Swing mechanics

**Objective:** To reinforce the mechanics of the lead hand moving toward the contact point during the swing.

**Equipment Needed:** Four baseballs, home plate, smaller bat and a screen or fence

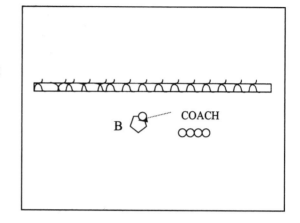

## COACH

- Demonstrate the swing with the lead hand before beginning the drill.

- Use an undersized bat 28 inches to 31 inches in length or have the players choke up to the top of the handgrip to control the bat with one hand.

- After modeling the toss, allow the players to pair up, and monitor both the hitter and tosser.

- Monitor the swing carefully, making sure the players do not adjust their swing to accommodate a one-handed swing.

## PLAYER

- Pair up: one hits while the other tosses.

- Each pair should have approximately four balls, preferably tennis or rag balls for safety.

- Start with both hands on the bat in a normal stance, then remove the back hand, placing it behind the back.

- Take 10 swings, paying close attention to the stance, hand position, stride and swing.

**NOTE:** Do not toss the balls quickly; give the hitter a chance to reset. It is important for the hitter to develop good habits. Use in conjunction with the regular "Flip-Toss Drill"; this will help break the swing down into smaller segments.

# 192. Flip-Toss Drill—Back Hand Swing

**Primary Skill:** Swing mechanics

**Objective:** To reinforce the mechanics of the back hand moving toward the contact point during the swing.

**Equipment Needed:** Four baseballs, home plate, smaller bat and screen or fence

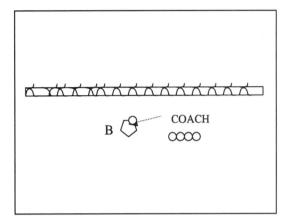

## COACH

- Demonstrate the swing with the back hand before beginning the drill.
- Use an undersized bat 28 inches to 31 inches in length or have the players choke up to the top of the handgrip to control the bat with one hand.
- After modeling the toss, allow the players to pair up, and monitor both the hitter and tosser.
- Monitor the swing carefully, making sure the players do not adjust their swing to accommodate a one-handed swing.

## PLAYER

- Pair up: one hits while the other tosses.
- Each pair should have approximately four balls, preferably tennis or rag balls for safety.
- Start with both hands on the bat in a normal stance, then remove the lead hand, placing it behind the back.
- Take 10 swings, paying close attention to the stance, hand position, stride and swing.

**NOTE:** Do not toss the balls quickly; give the hitter a chance to reset. It is important for the hitter to develop good habits. Use in conjunction with the regular "Flip-Toss Drill"; this will help break the swing down into smaller segments.

# 193. Flip-Toss–Slap Drill

**Primary Skill:** Hitting

**Objective:** To reinforce the hand movement toward the ball during the swing.

**Equipment Needed:** Six tennis balls or whiffle golf balls and a home plate

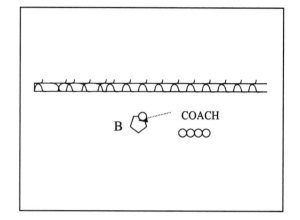

## COACH

- Demonstrate the swing with the front hand and then the back hand.
- After modeling toss, allow the players to pair up, and monitor both the hitter and tosser.
- Monitor the swing carefully, making sure the players do not adjust their swing to accommodate a one-handed swing.
- Make sure to use softer balls—hitters will be using a bare hand to hit the ball.

## PLAYER

- Pair up: one hits while the other tosses.
- Each pair should have approximately four balls, preferably tennis or rag balls for safety.
- Start with both hands in the regular bat position in a good stance, then place the hand not being used behind the back. When the toss is made, throw the hand to the ball, hitting the ball with the hand.
- Take 10 swings, five with the front hand and five with the back hand, paying close attention to the stance, hand position, stride and swing.

# 194. Flip-Toss–Two-Ball Drill

**Primary Skill:** Concentration

**Objective:** To develop concentration on the contact point during the swing.

**Equipment Needed:** Four tennis or rag balls, home plate, bat and a net or fence

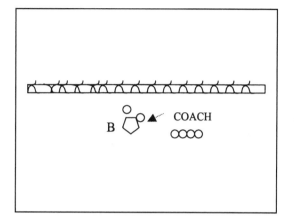

## COACH

- Explain the purpose and demonstrate the proper mechanics of the drill before starting.

- Set up the home plate with a batter and tosser with four balls. Model the correct tossing procedure by holding two balls at one time, then toss both balls to the batter.

- As the toss is being performed, call out the top or bottom ball. The batter will attempt to hit the ball that was called out. Make sure the tosser makes the call early enough for the batter to adjust to hit the correct ball.

- Have each batter take 10 repetitions before rotating with partner. Monitor each pair closely for the proper mechanics while tossing and swinging.

## PLAYER

- Pair up: one hits while the other tosses. Each pair should have approximately four balls, preferably tennis or rag balls for safety.

- Start in a good stance with the proper alignment at the plate. The tosser will start with two balls in hand, performing a good toss. During the initial movement of the toss, the tosser will call out either the top or bottom, indicating to the batter the ball to hit.

- Take 10 swings paying close attention to the stance, hand position, stride and swing before rotating with partner.

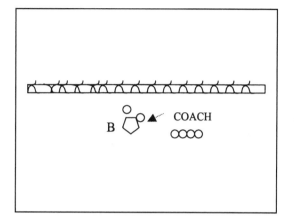

# 195. Flip-Toss–Numbered Ball Drill

**Primary Skill:** Concentration

**Objective:** To develop concentration on the contact point during the swing.

**Equipment Needed:** Four numbered tennis or rag balls, home plate, bat and a net or fence

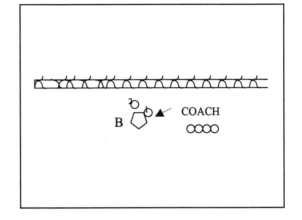

## COACH

- Explain the purpose and demonstrate the proper mechanics of the drill before starting.

- Set up the home plate with a batter and tosser with four numbered balls. Model the correct tossing procedure by holding two numbered balls at one time, then tossing both balls to the batter.

- As the toss is being performed, call out the number of the ball. The batter will attempt to hit the ball that was called out. Make sure the tosser makes the call early enough for the batter to adjust to hit the correct ball.

- Have each batter take 10 repetitions before rotating with partner. Monitor each pair closely for the proper mechanics while tossing and swinging.

## PLAYER

- Pair up: one hits while the other tosses. Each pair should have approximately four numbered balls, preferably tennis or rag balls for safety.

- Start in a good stance with the proper alignment at the plate. The tosser will start with two numbered balls in hand performing a good toss. During the initial movement of the toss, the tosser will call a number of one of the balls in hand, indicating which ball to hit.

- Take 10 swings paying close attention to the stance, hand position, stride and swing before rotating with partner.

# 196. Flip-Toss Drill from Behind

**Primary Skill:** Hand quickness

**Objective:** To develop hand quickness to the point of contact with the ball.

**Equipment Needed:** Four tennis or rag balls, bat, home plate and a net or fence

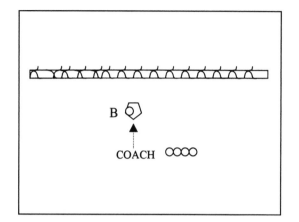

## COACH

- Demonstrate the proper tossing technique to players. This technique is very important—if the toss is not performed properly, the hitting repetitions will suffer.

- The tosser will be placed behind home plate close to the catcher's position. The tossing technique will not change, only the direction from which the ball is coming.

- After modeling a toss, allow the players to pair up, and monitor the hitter and the tosser.

## PLAYER

- Pair up: one hits while the other tosses from behind the plate. Keep the tossing technique the same even though the ball is coming from a different direction.

- Each pair should have approximately four balls, preferably tennis or rag balls for safety.

- Take 10 swings, paying close attention to the stance, hand position, stride and swing.

- Switch after 10 repetitions.

**NOTE:** Do not toss balls quickly; give hitter a chance to reset. It is important for the hitter to develop good habits.

# 197. Batting Tee Drill

**Primary Skill:** Hitting

**Objective:** To develop and reinforce the proper hitting mechanics.

**Equipment Needed:** Batting tees, four baseballs, screen or fence and a bat

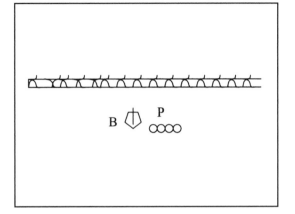

## COACH

- Demonstrate the proper swing prior to the start of drill and have the players pair up.
- Monitor the hitters carefully, making sure the players do not adjust their stance to accommodate the tee.

## PLAYER

- Pair up: one hits while the other places the ball on the tee.
- Each pair should have approximately four balls, preferably tennis or rag balls for safety.
- Start in a normal stance and distance from home plate; do not move away from the plate to extend the arms.
- Take 10 swings, paying close attention to the stance, hand position, stride and swing.

**NOTE:** This is not a race; give hitter a chance to reset. It is important for the hitter to develop good habits. If balls are not available, have the players swing at the top of the tee.

**HELPFUL HINTS:** Before using tees, tape around the top edge with duct tape or athletic tape. This will help stop the top from splitting along the edge.

# 198. Batting Tee—Lead Hand Swing

**Primary Skill:** Swing mechanics

**Objective:** To reinforce the mechanics of the lead hand moving toward the contact point during the swing.

**Equipment Needed:** Four baseballs, home plate, smaller bat and a screen or fence

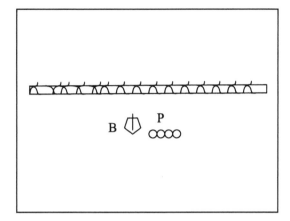

## COACH

- Demonstrate the swing using only the lead hand before beginning the drill.

- Use an undersized bat 28 inches to 31 inches in length or have the players choke up to the top of the handgrip to control the bat with one hand.

- Monitor the swing carefully, making sure the players do not adjust the swing to accommodate a one-handed swing.

## PLAYER

- Pair up: one hits while the other places the balls on the tee.

- Each pair should have approximately four balls, preferably tennis or rag balls for safety.

- Start with both hands on the bat in a normal stance and then remove the back hand, placing it behind the back. Complete the swing using the lead hand only. The swing mechanics are more important than contact with the ball.

- Take 10 swings, paying close attention to the stance, hand position, stride and swing.

# 199. Batting Tee—Back Hand Swing

**Primary Skill:** Swing mechanics

**Objective:** To reinforce the mechanics of the back hand moving toward the contact point during the swing.

**Equipment Needed:** Four baseballs, home plate, smaller bat and a screen or fence

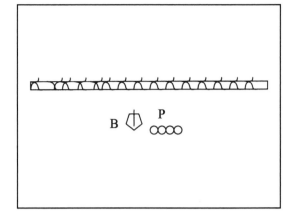

## COACH

- Demonstrate the swing using only the backhand before beginning the drill.

- Use undersized bat 28 inches to 31 inches in length or have the players choke up to the top of the handgrip to control the bat with one hand.

- Monitor the swing carefully, making sure the players do not adjust the swing to accommodate a one-handed swing.

## PLAYER

- Pair up: one hits while the other places the balls on the tee.

- Each pair should have approximately four balls, preferably tennis or rag balls for safety.

- Start with both hands on the bat in a normal stance and then remove the lead hand, placing it behind the back. Complete the swing using the back hand only. The swing mechanics are more important than contact with the ball.

- Take 10 swings, paying close attention to the stance, hand position, stride and swing.

# 200. Batting Tee Drill—Hitting the Inside Pitch

**Primary Skill:** Inside pitch swing

**Objective:** To practice the proper mechanics when hitting an inside pitch.

**Equipment Needed:** Batting tees, four baseballs, screen or fence and a bat

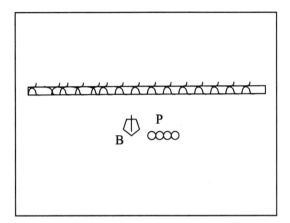

## COACH

- Demonstrate the proper swing for an inside pitch prior to the start of the drill and have the players pair up.

- Position the players at the batting tees to simulate an inside pitch by taking a half step closer to the plate and one full step closer to the catcher.

- Monitor the hitters carefully, making sure they do not adjust their stance to accommodate the tee.

## PLAYER

- Pair up: one hits while the other places balls on the tee.

- Each pair should have approximately four balls, preferably tennis or rag balls for safety.

- Start in a normal stance, moving a half step closer to home plate and one full step closer to the catcher. The tee positioning should simulate an inside pitch.

- Take 10 swings, paying close attention to the stance, hand position, stride and swing

# 201. Batting Tee Drill—Hitting the Outside Pitch

**Primary Skill:** Outside pitch swing

**Objective:** To practice the proper mechanics when hitting an outside pitch.

**Equipment Needed:** Batting tees, four baseballs, screen or fence and a bat.

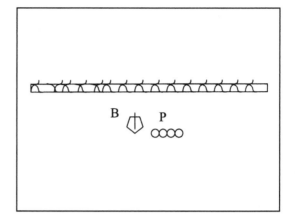

## COACH

- Demonstrate the proper swing for an inside pitch prior to the start of drill and have the players pair up.
- Position the players at the batting tees to simulate an outside pitch by taking one full step away from the catcher toward the front of home plate.
- Monitor the hitters carefully, making sure they do not adjust their stance to accommodate the tee.

## PLAYER

- Pair up: one hits while the other places balls on the tee.
- Each pair should have approximately four balls, preferably tennis or rag balls for safety.
- Start in a normal stance moving one full step away from the catcher toward the front of home plate. The tee positioning should simulate an outside pitch.
- Take 10 swings, paying close attention to the stance, hand position, stride and swing.

# 202. Double Tee Drill

**Primary Skill:** Swing mechanics

**Objective:** To practice the slight downward angle of the bat during the swing as the bat approaches the contact point.

**Equipment Needed:** Four baseballs, two batting tees and a net or fence

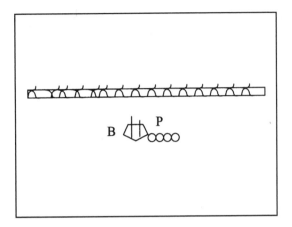

## COACH

- Demonstrate the proper swing prior to the start of drill and have the players pair up.
- Set up two batting tees, one in front of the other so that the tees are approximately a foot apart. The front tee should be 2 inches lower than the back tee.
- Monitor the hitters carefully, making sure the players do not adjust their stance to accommodate the tee.

## PLAYER

- Pair up: one hits while the other places the balls on the front tee.
- Each pair should have approximately four balls, preferably tennis or rag balls for safety.
- Start in a normal stance and distance from home plate; do not move away from the plate to extend the arms. The swing should have a slight downward angle to hit the ball on the front tee.
- Take 10 swings, paying close attention to the stance, hand position, stride and swing.

# 203. Walk-Through Drill

**Primary Skill:** Hitting

**Objective:** To reinforce keeping the weight and hands back prior to the swing.

**Equipment Needed:** Three baseballs, bat, batting tee and a net

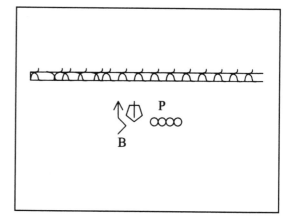

## COACH

- Explain and demonstrate the proper technique before beginning.

- Pair up the players with a batting tee with three baseballs and a bat. Start the batter two steps behind the plate compared to the normal stance position in the batter's box.

- The batter, from this position, steps through with back foot and then follows through with the other foot as the batter begins to swing at the ball on the batting tee.

- Check for the proper mechanics during the drill. Have each player take 10 repetitions before switching.

## PLAYER

- Stand with a bat two steps behind a batting tee and a ball on the tee. Step through with the back foot followed by the other foot to a swinging position.

- Once in a normal position next to the plate, use good mechanics to swing through the ball.

- Repeat drill 10 times before switching.

# 204. Drop Drill

**Primary Skill:** Hitting

**Objective:** To develop quick hands through the strike zone by using the proper swing technique.

**Equipment Needed:** Home plate, four baseballs, a bat and a screen or fence

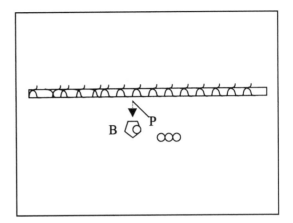

## COACH

- Demonstrate the proper drop technique, emphasizing safety. Also, emphasize an initial upward movement of the arm to help the hitter prepare for the swing with an initial load.
- After modeling the drop, allow the players to pair up.
- Monitor the hitters carefully, making sure the players do not adjust their stance. It's important the hitter maintains a compact swing.

## PLAYER

- Pair up: one hits while the other drops the ball into the strike zone.
- Each pair should have approximately four balls, preferably tennis or rag balls for safety.
- Start in a normal stance; prepare for the swing by loading when your partner gives an initial upward arm movement.
- Take 10 swings, paying close attention to the stance, hand position, stride and swing.

# 205. Drop Drill—Whiffle Golf Balls

**Primary Skill:** Hitting

**Objective:** To develop quick hands through the strike zone by using the proper swing technique.

**Equipment Needed:** Home plate, four baseballs, three-foot broomstick and a screen or fence

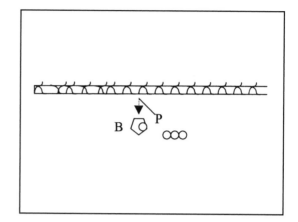

## COACH

- Demonstrate the proper drop technique, emphasizing safety. Also, emphasize an initial upward movement of the arm to help the hitter prepare to swing with an initial load.

- After modeling the drop, allow the players to pair up. Substitute the golf whiffle balls and broomstick into the drill.

- Monitor the hitters carefully, making sure players do not adjust their stance. It's important the hitter maintains a compact swing.

## PLAYER

- Pair up: one hits while the other drops the ball into the strike zone.

- Each pair should have approximately four golf whiffle balls and a three-foot broomstick.

- Start in a normal stance; prepare for the swing by loading when your partner gives an initial upward arm movement.

- Take 10 swings, paying close attention to the stance, hand position, stride and swing.

# 206. Bounce Drill

**Primary Skill:** Hitting

**Objective:** To reinforce keeping the hands and weight back during the swing.

**Equipment Needed:** Four tennis balls, net or fence and a hard surface

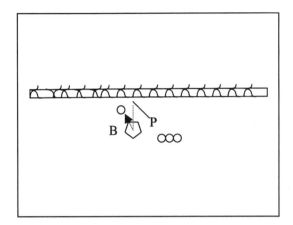

## COACH

- Demonstrate the proper drop technique, emphasizing the bounce. Also, emphasize an initial upward movement of the arm to help the hitter prepare for the swing with an initial load. Remind the hitters to keep the hands and weight back until the ball bounces off the ground.

- After modeling the drop, allow the players to pair up.

- Monitor the hitters carefully, making sure the players do not adjust their stance. It's important the hitter maintains a compact swing.

## PLAYER

- Pair up: one hits while the other drops the ball into the strike zone. Each pair should have approximately four tennis balls.

- Start in a normal stance; prepare for the swing by stepping when your partner gives an initial upward arm movement. After the ball is dropped, keep your hands and weight back, waiting to hit the ball on the bounce off the ground.

- Take 10 swings, paying close attention to the stance, hand position, stride and swing.

# 207. Whiffle Golf Ball Drill

**Primary Skill:** Hitting

**Objective:** To develop focus and concentration on the ball through the strike zone.

**Equipment Needed:** Six whiffle golf balls, a bat and a home plate

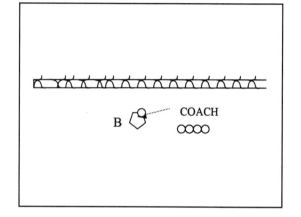

## COACH

- Set up the flip-toss drill using the golf whiffle balls as a substitute for other balls and a regular bat.
- Have the players perform the flip-toss, emphasizing the proper swing mechanics.
- Monitor the drill closely, providing corrections and encouragement when necessary.

## PLAYER

- Pair up with another player, setting up the flip-toss drill using golf whiffle balls and a regular bat.
- The toss to the batter is extremely important to the success of the drill. Do not rush the batter; allow time for the batter to reset in between tosses.
- Focus on the ball through the contact point; emphasize the head remaining on the ball keeping the front side closed.
- Take 10 good swings before rotating with other players.

# 208. Whiffle Golf Ball Drill—Broom Stick

**Primary Skill:** Hitting

**Objective:** To develop focus and concentration on the ball through the strike zone.

**Equipment Needed:** Six whiffle golf balls, three-foot broom stick and a home plate

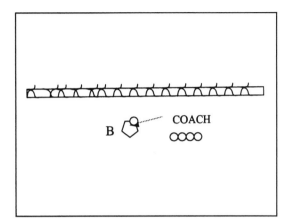

## COACH

- Set up the flip-toss drill using the golf whiffle balls as a substitute for other balls and a broomstick approximately three feet long.
- Have the players perform the flip-toss, emphasizing the proper swing mechanics.
- Monitor the drill closely, providing corrections and encouragement when necessary.

## PLAYER

- Pair up with another player, setting up the flip-toss drill using golf whiffle balls and a broomstick approximately three feet long.
- The toss to the batter is extremely important to the success of the drill. Do not rush the batter; allow time for the batter to reset in between tosses.
- Focus on the ball through the contact point; emphasize the head remaining on the ball keeping the front side closed.
- Take 10 good swings before rotating with other players.

# 209. Dry Swing

**Primary Skill:** Hitting

**Objective:** To reinforce the proper hitting mechanics, which include the stance, step, swing and rhythm.

**Equipment Needed:** Bat

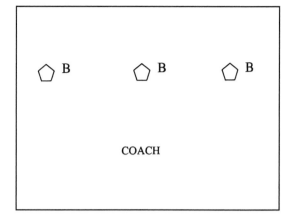

## COACH

- Safety is most important; make sure other players are clear of swinging area.
- Place the batters in an area clear of other players. Have the player perform the swing as if they are in the batter's box.
- Use prior to a game, during batting practice or in the on-deck circle, and to evaluate the player's swing, checking for the proper mechanics.
- This can also be used as a confidence builder and a warm-up drill prior to the game.

## PLAYER

- Perform the swing with a bat against air clear of other players, focusing on the proper fundamentals involved in the mechanics of the swing.
- This is a great opportunity to self-evaluate your swing.

**NOTE:** Incorporate this with other drills during a regular practice, especially preseason.

# 210. Compact Swing

**Primary Skill:** Hitting

**Objective:** To develop and reinforce the hand and arm position involved in creating a compact swing.

**Equipment Needed:** Bat, net and a screen or fence

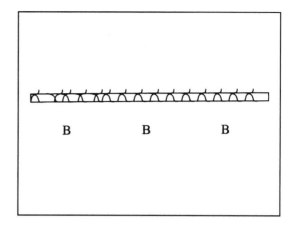

## COACH

- Demonstrate the compact swing to the players before the drill.
- Emphasize keeping the back arm next to the rib cage; this will help keep the swing compact. Also, emphasize throwing hands at the ball—the back arm will extend as the swing progresses through the strike zone.
- Monitor the drill, evaluating the swing giving positive feedback.

## PLAYER

- Take a bat and align a bat length away from the net. Get into a good batting stance parallel to the net. Perform the swing with good mechanics so the bat does not hit the net.
- Perform the drill as many times as needed. This is a good warm-up drill prior to the game or batting practice.

**NOTE:** This drill is very good for helping the players that like to extend the arms on the swing. This cures swinging around the strike zone instead of through it.

# 211. Mime Bunt

**Primary Skill:** Bunting

**Objective:** To practice and reinforce the proper movement, body position and technique involved in bunting.

**Equipment Needed:** Bat

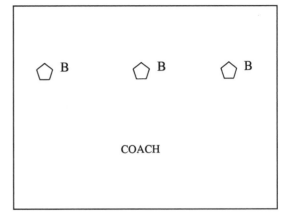

## COACH

- Demonstrate the bunting technique prior to the start of the drill.
- Align the batters equal distance apart facing the pitcher or coach as the setup for the drill. The coach cues the batters to get into the bunt position by using a pitcher's windup. The balls are not being thrown during this drill.
- Evaluate timing and bunt mechanics during the drill.

## PLAYER

- Get a bat to perform this drill, aligning far enough apart from other players.
- Focus on the pitcher or coach waiting for the proper time to get into a bunt-ready position.
- Reset after each repetition.

# 212. Bunt Teams

**Primary Skill:** Bunting

**Objective:** To practice and reinforce the proper movement, body position and technique, as well as the bunt itself.

**Equipment Needed:** Four balls, a bat and a home plate

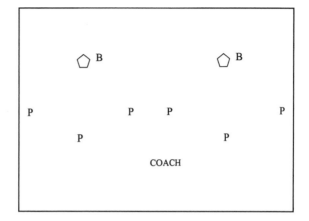

## COACH

- Demonstrate the proper bunting mechanics prior to the start of the drill.

- Set up teams of four players with enough room to pitch from 15 to 20 feet with four tennis balls and home plates.

- Monitor each team for the proper bunting technique and every pitching motion to ensure each batter can get the proper timing. Emphasize batter preparation before the pitcher releases the ball.

- The two other players will help field balls; also rotate to the pitcher and batter positions.

- Initially, have the players work on the bunt mechanics and contact with the ball and then progress to two balls bunted down the first and third base lines.

## PLAYER

- Create teams with three other players with four balls and a home plate. One player becomes the bunter while another becomes the pitcher, the other two field bunts.

- The pitcher gives the batter a full pitching motion, throwing the ball half-speed. The batter focuses on timing, the proper bunting mechanics and making contact with the ball.

- Rotate after 5 to 10 repetitions.

# 213. Bucket Drill

**Primary Skill:** Bunting

**Objective:** To develop the skill of bunting the ball down the first and third base lines.

**Equipment Needed:** Six baseballs, two buckets, a bat and a home plate

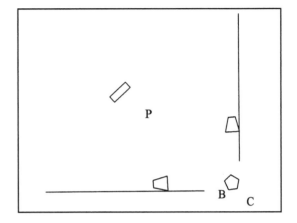

## COACH

- Demonstrate the proper bunt technique prior to starting the drill.
- Set up the drill with a batter at home plate, two buckets placed along the first and third base lines and a pitcher 30 feet away.
- The pitcher will give the batter a windup or stretch motion prior to pitching the ball. On the pitch, have the batter get into good body position to bunt the ball down the first or third base line into the buckets.
- Monitor each batter's mechanics carefully during the drill. Have each batter take 5 to 10 repetitions before rotating.

## PLAYER

- Start next to home plate in a good hitting stance. On the pitcher's motion, move to the bunt position.
- The goal is to bunt the ball either down the first or the third base line into the buckets.
- Take 5 to 10 repetitions before rotating.

# 214. Close-Quarter Batting Practice

**Primary Skill:** Hitting

**Objective:** To make batting practice more efficient.

**Equipment Needed:** Pitching screen, bag of baseballs, bats, home plate and a batting cage or field

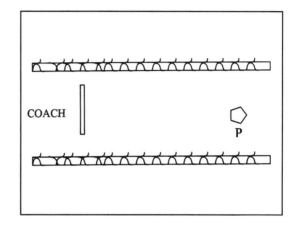

## COACH

- Set the pitching screen about half the normal distance. This helps efficiency and effectiveness by controlling the batting practice, bunts and the number of swings.
- Use the pitchers on occasion; this will help them find the strike zone more consistently.
- Also, the speed of the pitches can be adjusted without extra strain on the arm.
- The throwing arm will last longer during batting practice and on a daily basis.

## PLAYER

- Normal batting practice—follow the coach's instructions for bunts, the number of swings, etc.
- Focus on the pitcher's movement and release point, as well as working on timing.

**NOTE:** Vary speeds during batting practice to help batters adjust to off-speed pitches, such as curve balls and change-ups.

# 215. Batting Practice with a Purpose

**Primary Skill:** Hitting

**Objective:** To reinforce hitting mechanics, also to develop situational thinking while hitting.

**Equipment Needed:** Pitching screen, bag of baseballs, bats, home plate and a batting cage or field

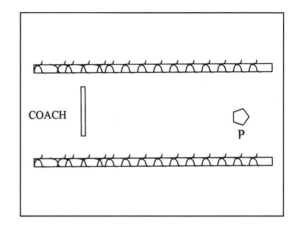

## COACH

• Use at a normal distance or close-quarter batting practice. Also, use either the batting cage or the diamond. When using the diamond, the batters can become base runners.

• Give the batter the situation before each pitch:
  —Sacrifice bunt.
  —Hit and run.
  —Swing away.
  —Runner on third base with less than two outs: hit a fly ball to the outfield.
  —Bunt for a base hit.

• Using runners helps create a more realistic situation.

• Give each player a few repetitions in each situation; during pregame, cut down on repetitions.

## PLAYER

• Follow the coach's instruction for bunts, the number of swings, etc.

• Focus on the situations and the pitcher's movement and release point, as well as working on timing.

**NOTE:** Post the batting situations on the backstop to prepare the players when taking repetitions.

# SECTION 7

# BASE RUNNING

*Success is not so much achievement as achieving. Refuse to join the cautious crowd that plays not to lose—play to win.*

—DAVID J. MAHONEY

# 216. Crossover Drill

**Primary Skill:** The crossover step

**Objective:** To develop the proper initial step from a lead stance when advancing to another base.

**Equipment Needed:** None

```
    P    P    P    P

    P    P    P    P


         COACH
```

## COACH

- Demonstrate the proper crossover step before beginning the drill.

- Place players in lines that are four across and two or three deep approximately 8 to 10 feet apart in a good lead stance.

- Stand in front of the players in a pitcher's stretch position. Give the players an initial movement to home so the crossover step can be performed.

- The players will only take the initial crossover step and then reset. Continue through the drill for approximately 10 repetitions.

- Monitor the players' mechanics during the initial step, making sure bodies stay low.

## PLAYER

- Align in four across and two to three deep approximately 8 to 10 feet apart in a good lead stance.

- Watch the coach to pick up the movement to home from the stretch position. On the coach's movement, take the initial crossover step toward the next base.

- After the initial step, reset for the next repetition.

# 217. Sliding Drill

**Primary Skill:** Sliding

**Objective:** To develop and practice the sliding technique when approaching a base.

**Equipment Needed:** Two blankets and one base

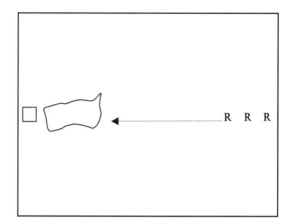

## COACH

- Demonstrate the proper mechanics before beginning.
- Set up the drill in the gym by placing a throw-down base on the floor with two blankets 10 to 15 feet in front of the base.
- Start the players approximately 30 feet from the base, then have them run toward the bag and slide on the blankets in front of the base.
- Have the players take five repetitions each, monitoring each repetition closely.

## PLAYER

- Align approximately 30 feet from the base in a good stance.
- On the coach's signal take a good crossover step running toward the base. Use good sliding mechanics to slide on the blankets in front of the base.
- Move to the back of the line after each repetition. Take five repetitions during the drill.

# 218. Tagging Up Drill—First and Second Base

**Primary Skill:** Baserunning

**Objective:** To practice tagging up on a fly ball hit to the outfield.

**Equipment Needed:** Three bases, a fungo bat, six baseballs and gloves

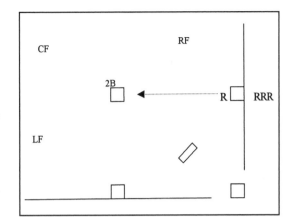

## COACH

- Demonstrate the proper mechanics of the drill before beginning.

- Place the runners at either first or second base. Let them take a normal lead at the bag. Set up the outfielders and an infielder to cover the bag to which the runner is moving.

- Hit fly balls to the outfield having the runners tag on the caught ball.

- Give each runner three repetitions and monitor techniques closely, providing encouragement when appropriate.

## PLAYER

- Align at either first or second base with a normal lead and in a good stance.

- Wait for the coach to hit a fly ball to the outfield. If the ball is in view, tag on the catch; if it cannot be seen, rely on the coach's verbal cue to tag.

- Take three repetitions before rotating with the other players.

# 219. Tagging Up Drill—Third Base

**Primary Skill:** Baserunning

**Objective:** To practice tagging up on a fly ball hit to the outfield.

**Equipment Needed:** One base, a home plate, a fungo bat, six baseballs and gloves

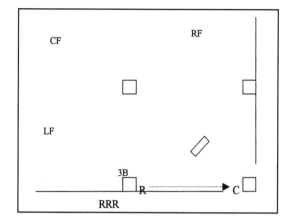

## COACH

- Demonstrate the proper mechanics before beginning.

- Place the runners at third base. Have them take a normal lead at the bag. Set up the outfielders and use a catcher to cover home plate and a coach to give instructions at third base.

- Hit fly balls to the outfield having the runner tag on the catch.

- Give each runner three repetitions and monitor techniques closely, providing encouragement when appropriate.

## PLAYER

- Align at third base with a normal lead and in a good stance.

- Wait for the coach to hit a fly ball to the outfield. Go back to the bag and listen for the third base coach's verbal cue to go.

- Take three repetitions before rotating with other players.

# 220. Tip-Off Drill—Right-Handed Pitcher

**Primary Skill:** Baserunning

**Objective:** To practice recognizing signals from a right-handed pitcher that tip off the base runner.

**Equipment Needed:** Three baseballs, two bases and gloves

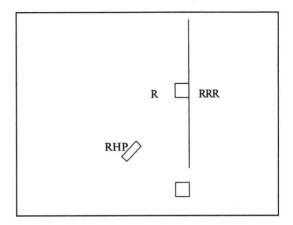

## COACH

- Explain and demonstrate the proper mechanics before beginning the drill.
- Place the runners at first base with a first baseman covering the bag and a right-handed pitcher on the mound.
- The pitcher will start from the stretch position, performing the motion with the option of making a move to first base or to home. The runner takes a normal lead in a balanced stance focusing on the pitcher's motion.
- Monitor the runner's lead and stance, making corrections as well as providing encouragement when appropriate.

## PLAYER

- Align at the first base bag taking a normal lead with a good balanced stance, focusing on the pitcher. Another player covers the first base bag holding the runner close.
- Watch for tip-offs given by the right-handed pitcher when making a move to the first base bag, such as lifting the right heel when coming to first base or lifting the left heel when going home.
- Remain in a balanced stance until the pitcher makes a move. If the pitcher goes home, take a crossover step toward second base. If the pitcher makes a move toward first base, take a crossover step and dive back to first base.
- Rotate after every repetition.

# 221. Stealing Drill

**Primary Skill:** Baserunning

**Objective:** To practice taking a lead and stealing a base.

**Equipment Needed:** Three baseballs, two bases and gloves

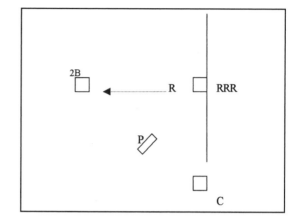

## COACH

- Explain and demonstrate the proper mechanics before beginning the drill.

- Place the runners at first base and place a first baseman, a second baseman, a catcher and a pitcher at their respective positions.

- The pitcher will start from the stretch position, performing the motion with the option of making a move to first base or to home. The runner takes a normal lead in a balanced stance, focusing on the pitcher's motion. When the pitcher throws home, the runner attempts to steal second and the catcher will make a throw to second base attempting to throw out the runner.

- Monitor the runner's lead and stance, making corrections as well as providing encouragement when appropriate.

## PLAYER

- Align at the first base bag taking a normal lead with a good balanced stance, focusing on the pitcher. Three other players play first base, second base and catcher.

- Watch for tip-offs given by the pitcher when making a move to the first base bag.

- Remain in a balanced stance until the pitcher makes a move. If the pitcher goes home, take a crossover step to steal second base. If the pitcher makes a move toward first base, take a crossover step and dive back to first base.

- Rotate after every repetition.

# 222. Tip-Off Drill—Left-Handed Pitcher

**Primary Skill:** Baserunning

**Objective:** To practice recognizing signals from a left-handed pitcher that tip off the base runner.

**Equipment Needed:** Three baseballs, two bases and gloves

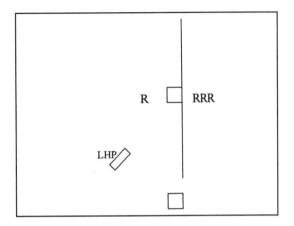

## COACH

- Explain and demonstrate the proper mechanics before beginning the drill.

- Place the runners at first base with a first baseman covering the bag and a left-handed pitcher on the mound.

- The pitcher will start from the stretch position, performing the motion with the option of making a move to first base or to home. The runner takes a normal lead in a balanced stance, focusing on the pitcher's motion.

- Monitor the runner's lead and stance, making corrections as well as providing encouragement when appropriate.

## PLAYER

- Align at the first base bag taking a normal lead with a good balanced stance, focusing on the left-handed pitcher. Another player covers the first base bag holding the runner close.

- Watch for tip-offs given by the left-handed pitcher when making a move to the first base bag, such as the lead foot crossing behind the pitching rubber or the lead foot stepping toward first base.

- Remain in a balanced stance until the pitcher makes a move. If the pitcher goes home, take a crossover step toward second base. If the pitcher makes a move toward first base, take a crossover step and dive back to first base.

- Rotate after every repetition.

# 223. First Base Turn Drill—Veer Out

**Primary Skill:** Baserunning

**Objective:** To reinforce the proper mechanics while making a turn at first base.

**Equipment Needed:** One base

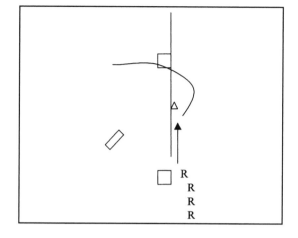

## COACH

• Explain and demonstrate the proper mechanics before starting the drill.

• Place runners at home plate in a line. Each will take a turn running to first base and veering to the right when approximately 20 feet from the bag to make the turn at first base. Place a cone or other type of marker at the spot the runners should veer out.

• Emphasize to the runners to hit the front inside corner of the first base bag when making the turn and to make an aggressive turn at the bag, always thinking of going to second base.

• Monitor the runners closely during the drill, making corrections when needed. Have each runner take three to five repetitions.

## PLAYER

• Align at home plate waiting for the coach's signal to begin running.

• On the signal, run toward first, veering out approximately 20 feet before the bag. Hit the bag on the front inside corner when rounding toward second base.

• After rounding the bag, check for the ball coming back into the infield, only then retreat to first base.

# 224. First Base Turn Drill—Extra Base Hit

**Primary Skill:** Baserunning

**Objective:** To reinforce the proper mechanics while making a turn at first base.

**Equipment Needed:** Two bases

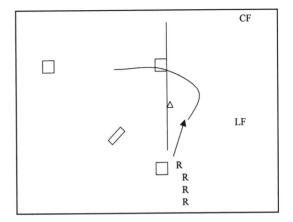

## COACH

- Explain and demonstrate the proper mechanics before starting the drill.

- Place runners at home plate in a single line. Each will take a turn running to first base, veering out to the right immediately upon leaving the batter's box so they can make the turn at first base.

- Emphasize to the runners to hit the front inside corner of the first base bag and make an aggressive turn at the bag, always thinking of taking an extra base.

- Monitor the runners closely during the drill, making corrections when needed. Have each runner take three to five repetitions.

## PLAYER

- Align at home plate waiting for the coach's signal to begin running.

- On the coach's signal, run toward first, veering out to the right immediately upon leaving the batter's box to make an aggressive turn at first base, thinking of extra bases. Hit the bag on the front inside corner when rounding toward second base.

# 225. First Base Turn Drill—Aggressive Turns

**Primary Skill:** Baserunning

**Objective:** To reinforce the proper mechanics while making an aggressive turn at first base.

**Equipment Needed:** Two bases, a fungo bat, six baseballs and gloves

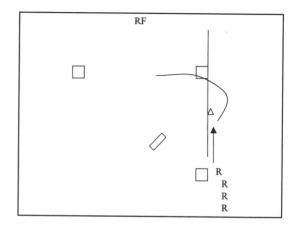

## COACH

• Explain and demonstrate the proper mechanics before starting the drill.

• Place runners at home plate in a single line. Each will take a turn running toward first base, veering out to the right when approximately 20 feet from the bag to make an aggressive turn at first base, going about 30 feet toward second base while watching the ball. Emphasize to the runners to hit the front inside corner of the first base bag.

• Incorporate outfielders into the drill to give runners a realistic look when rounding the first base bag. Hit balls to the outfielders and have them either field the balls cleanly or bobble the balls.

• Monitor the runners closely during the drill, making corrections when needed. Have each runner take three to five repetitions.

## PLAYER

• Align at home plate waiting for the coach's signal to begin running.

• On the coach's signal, run toward first, veering out to the right when approximately 20 feet from the bag to make an aggressive turn at first base. Go about 30 feet toward second base while watching the ball. Hit the bag on the front inside corner when rounding toward second base.

• After rounding the bag, check for the ball being fielded by the outfielders; when the ball comes back to the infield, retreat to the first base bag.

# 226. Circuit Running

**Primary Skill:** Base running, conditioning

**Objective:** To reinforce proper base running, while incorporating conditioning.

**Equipment Needed:** Three bases and a home plate

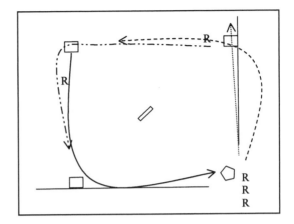

## COACH

· Talk through and demonstrate proper base running. From home to first base, from home to second base, from home to third base, from second base to home and from first base to third base.

· Explain sequence of running:

—Home to first (jog back) ·····························➤

—Home to second base (stay at second base) ------------➤

—Second base to home ————————➤

—Home to first base (stay at first base) ·····························➤

—First base to third base ---·--·--·--·--·-➤

· Monitor each runner carefully; have the runners wait until the man in front is halfway down the baseline before starting. This helps the coach focus on the runner at the base.

## PLAYER

· Listen for the running sequence from the coach.

· Use the proper technique when running to each base; use good angles when taking more than one base.

# 227. Leads at First Base

**Primary Skill:** Taking a lead

**Objective:** To reinforce and practice taking leads off first base and recognizing the pitcher's initial movement.

**Equipment Needed:** Three baseballs, gloves and a base

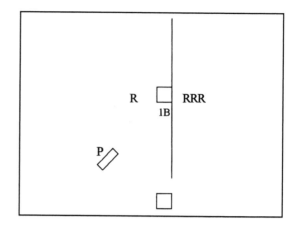

## COACH

- Set up in the gym or on the field. Talk through and demonstrate the lead technique, as well as pointing out visual cues from the pitcher: right-handed pitcher—back heel movement; left-handed pitcher—lead foot.

- Use more than one runner during the drill movement; stack the runners—each runner needs to be able to see the pitcher.

- Set the pitcher on the mound in the stretch position, alternate between right- and left-handed pitchers and have the first baseman cover the bag.

## PLAYER

- Line up at first base to take repetitions, taking leads at first base with a live pitcher.

- Take a lead at first base keeping an eye on the pitcher and looking for visual clues. Maintain good technique during the lead. If the pitcher makes a move toward home, take steps toward second base; if the pitcher makes a move toward first base, get back to the first base bag.

- The pitcher will vary the delivery home and/or pick-off moves to first base.

# 228. Leads at Second Base

**Primary Skill:** Taking a lead

**Objective:** To reinforce and practice taking leads off second base as well as visual cues from the pitcher.

**Equipment Needed:** Three baseballs, gloves and bases

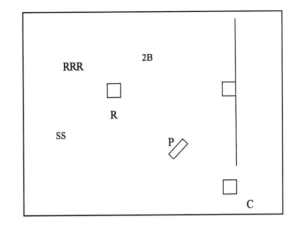

## COACH

- Set up in the gym or on the field with the second baseman, shortstop, pitcher and catcher.
- Talk through and demonstrate the lead technique prior to the drill.
- Have the runners positioned at second base, using one at a time. Use the same technique that was used at first base.
- Use a third base coach to communicate with the runner: the runner watches the second baseman while the coach watches the shortstop.

## PLAYER

- Align at second base, one runner taking repetitions at a time, so either the second baseman and shortstop can cover.
- Use same technique for leads at first base, focusing on the pitcher but also being aware of the second baseman. As the pitcher makes a move toward home plate, a secondary lead toward third base needs to take place.
- If the pitcher makes a move toward second, use good technique to get back to the bag.

**NOTE:** Incorporate pick-off moves for the pitchers, as well as base coverage for the second baseman and shortstop.

# 229. Leads at Third Base

**Primary Skill:** Base running, leads

**Objective:** To reinforce and practice running leads from third, as well as quickly recognizing a fly ball or a ground ball.

**Equipment Needed:** A base, three baseballs and gloves

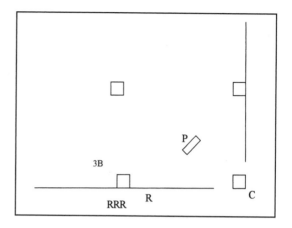

## COACH

- Set up in the gym or on the field with the third baseman, pitcher and catcher.
- Talk through and demonstrate the technique prior to the drill.
- The pitcher can pitch from both the windup and stretch; add the batter after the runners go through a few repetitions.
- Rotate all the players through drill.

## PLAYER

- Pitcher and catcher are live for proper timing.
- Third baseman plays normal position with man on third base.
- Runner starts about a foot off third in foul territory; as pitcher begins to deliver ball to plate, runner starts jogging toward plate.
- If the ball is not hit, runner gets right back to bag. On a ball hit in the air, the runner gets back to the bag to tag. On a ball hit on the ground, runner continues home.

**NOTE:** Incorporate batter to develop better timing and feel for batted ball.

# 230. Home to Second Base

**Primary Skill:** Baserunning

**Objective:** To practice running from home to second base with the first base coach's direction.

**Equipment Needed:** Two bases

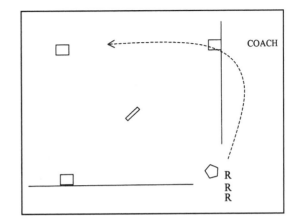

## COACH

- Set up in the gym or on the field with the first base coach giving directions on whether to stop or go.

- Talk through and demonstrate the runner's path prior to the start of the drill.

- Monitor each runner for the proper technique when rounding first base.

## PLAYER

- Start at home plate, sprint thinking second base while listening for the coach's communication.

- If the coach communicates to stop at first, make the turn, look for the ball, then hustle back to first. If the coach communicates to go, continue to hustle to second.

- After the repetition, jog back to home plate.

# 231. Home to Third Base

**Primary Skill:** Baserunning

**Objective:** To practice running from home plate to third base with base coach's instructions.

**Equipment Needed:** Three bases

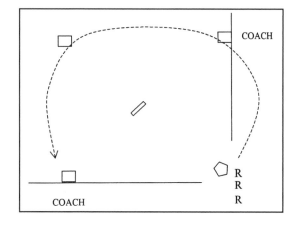

## COACH

- Set up in the gym if there is enough room or on the field, with base coaches at first and third giving instructions.

- Monitor each runner's technique while running the bases.

## PLAYER

- Start at home, sprint to first base, listen for the first base coach's instructions as you run toward and around first base.

- Pick up on the third base coach when approaching second base, watching for a stop or go signal.

**NOTE:** This also gives the coaches practice in making quick decisions with the runners moving on base.

# 232. Second Base to Home

**Primary Skill:** Baserunning

**Objective:** To practice running from second base to home with a coach's instructions.

**Equipment Needed:** Three bases and a home plate

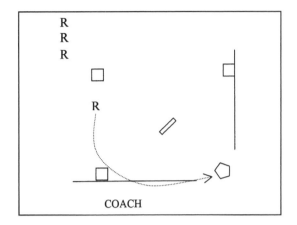

## COACH

- Set up in the gym if there is enough room or on the field, with the coach giving instructions from the third base coach's box. Signal the runners to stop at third or to continue home.

- Monitor each runner's technique while running the bases.

## PLAYER

- Start at second, sprint toward home and listen for the third base coach's instructions to and around third base, watching for a stop or go signal.

- The runners need to sprint; do not anticipate the coach's signal.

**NOTE:** All base running drills are a great opportunity to combine technique practice with conditioning.

# 233. First Base to Third Base

**Primary Skill:** Baserunning

**Objective:** To practice running from first to third base with a coach's instructions.

**Equipment Needed:** Three bases and a home plate

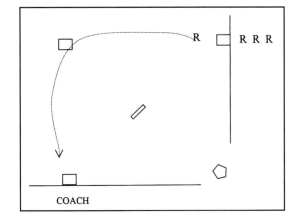

## COACH

• Set up in the gym if there is enough room or on the field, with the coach giving instructions from the third base coach's box. Signal the runners to stop at second or to continue to third base.

• Monitor each runner's technique while running bases.

## PLAYER

• Start at first, sprint toward third base and listen for instructions of the third base coach to and around second base, watching for a stop or go signal.

• Runners need to sprint; do not anticipate the coach's signal.

**NOTE:** All base running drills are a great opportunity to combine technique practice with conditioning.

# 234. First and Third Drill

**Primary Skill:** Baserunning

**Objective:** To practice the timing of the runner on third base breaking toward home on the catcher's throw to second base.

**Equipment Needed:** Six baseballs, three bases, home plate and catcher's gear

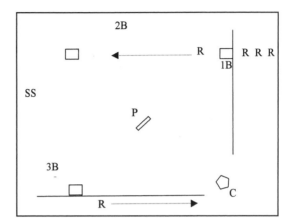

## COACH

- Explain the purpose of the drill and demonstrate the timing of the break home before beginning.

- Set up a regular infield with a pitcher and a catcher, with runners on first and third base. The pitcher will begin the drill from the stretch position, either making a move to first base or a throw home.

- When the pitcher throws home, the runner on first base tries to steal second base and the runner on third base waits to see if the ball is going to second base or being cut off before breaking for home.

- Rotate the runners from first base to third base before rotating out of the drill. Monitor the timing of the base runner on third closely.

## PLAYER

- Align as runners at first base and third base, taking a proper lead in a good stance and focusing on the pitcher.

- When on first base, wait for the pitcher to throw home before attempting to steal second base. If on third, watch the catcher's throw to second base, making sure it is not cut off, before breaking to home plate.

- Rotate from a first base runner to a third base runner to out of the drill.

# 235. Bunt and Run Drill

**Primary Skill:** Baserunning

**Objective:** To practice the base runner's timing during a bunt play.

**Equipment Needed:** Six baseballs, two bases, a home plate, a bat, batting helmets, gloves and a screen

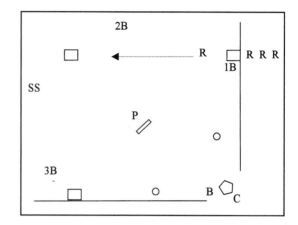

## COACH

• Explain the mechanics of the drill before beginning.

• Place a pitcher on the mound throwing from the stretch position, a batter at the plate and a runner at first or second base. Use a screen behind the batter to stop the pitches; incorporate a catcher later.

• The batter will attempt to lay a bunt down the first or third base line. The runner will take a crossover step on the throw home, but will wait until the bunt is on the ground to continue to the next base.

• Monitor the runner's timing during this drill. Another coach can monitor the pitcher's mechanics as well as the batter's technique on the bunt.

## PLAY

• Align at first or second base as a runner taking a lead in a good stance, focusing on the pitcher.

• As the pitcher throws home, take a crossover step watching to see the bunt on the ground. When the bunt is on the ground, continue moving toward the next base.

• After taking a repetition, go to the back of the runner's line.

# 236. Squeeze Drill

**Primary Skill:** Baserunning

**Objective:** To practice the base runner's timing during a squeeze bunt play.

**Equipment Needed:** Six baseballs, two bases, home plate, a bat, batting helmets, gloves and a screen

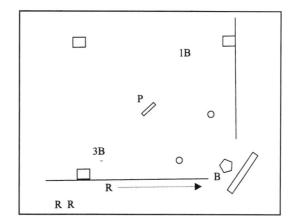

## COACH

- Explain the mechanics of the drill before beginning.

- Place a pitcher on the mound throwing from the windup or stretch position, a batter at the plate and runners at third base. Use a screen behind the batter to stop the pitches; incorporate a catcher later.

- The batter will attempt to lay a bunt down the first or third base line. The runner will take a crossover step on the throw home, but will wait until the bunt is on the ground to continue toward home plate.

- Monitor the runner's timing during this drill. Another coach can monitor the pitcher's mechanics as well as the batter's technique on the bunt.

## PLAY

- Align at third base as a runner taking a lead in a good stance, focusing on the pitcher.

- As the pitcher throws home, take a crossover step watching to see the bunt on the ground. When the bunt is on the ground, continue moving toward home plate.

- After taking a repetition, go to the back of the runner's line.

# 237. Suicide Squeeze Drill

**Primary Skill:** Baserunning

**Objective:** To practice the base runner's timing during a suicide squeeze play.

**Equipment Needed:** Six baseballs, two bases, home plate, a bat, batting helmets, gloves and a screen

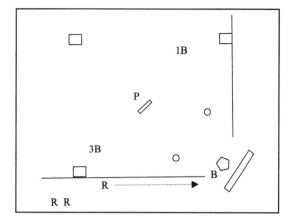

## COACH

- Explain the mechanics of the drill before beginning.

- Place a pitcher on the mound throwing from the windup or stretch position, a batter at the plate and runners at third base. Use a screen behind the batter to stop the pitches; incorporate a catcher later.

- The batter will attempt to lay a bunt down in fair territory. As soon as the pitcher starts the movement toward home plate, the runner will take off toward home plate in full sprint.

- Monitor the runner's timing during this drill. Another coach can monitor the pitcher's mechanics as well as the batter's technique on the bunt.

## PLAY

- Align at third base as a runner taking a lead in a good stance, focusing on the pitcher.

- As the pitcher throws toward home, take off toward home plate in full sprint.

- After taking a repetition, go to the back of the runner's line.

**NOTE:** During a game situation, remind the runners to slide across the front corner of the plate.

# 238. Two Outs—Full Count Drill

**Primary Skill:** Baserunning

**Objective:** To practice the two outs, full count situation with base runners.

**Equipment Needed:** Three baseballs, gloves, three bases and a screen

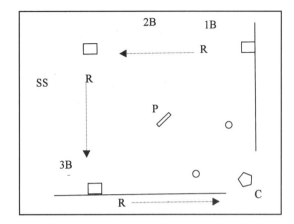

## COACH

- Explain the proper technique and the situation before beginning the drill.

- Place runners at either first base, first and second base or load the bases. Put a pitcher on the mound pitching from the windup or the stretch position. Incorporate a catcher and a batter at a later time.

- On the start of the pitcher's motion toward home plate, the runners start running.

- Monitor the runner's timing during this drill. Another coach can monitor the pitcher's mechanics.

## PLAYER

- Align at either first base, second base or third the base, taking a lead in a good stance, focusing on the pitcher.

- On the start of the pitcher's motion toward home plate, start to run, watching for the ball to be put in play.

- After taking a repetition, go to the back of the runner's line.